Praise for *The Heart of Leadershi*

"Lisa's book is a guide to spiritual leadership, but also followership. It teaches us all to follow our highest calling and pay attention to what we learn. By modeling our devotion to a higher purpose, we help those who will be the leaders of the future."
~Rev. Rosalyn L. Bruyere, internationally acclaimed healer and medicine woman; author of *Wheels of Light*

"This flowing read is for everyone who wishes to understand the call to lead from within, in its being as much as in the doing. From gratitude to intention, from self-care to planning, Lisa unfolds an easy-to-follow pathway to transform an event that's "good", into a "lovely" and nourishing experience for mind, body and spirit – and proves that the key to effectiveness in leadership is in the fulfillment of the soul."
~Mariabruna Sirabella, founder of the School of the Origins; SoulCollage® Lead Trainer

"I devoured this book. It was informative and enjoyable to read, and I found many things I wish I had practiced, and others that I did. I encourage all women to read this book, because we're all facilitators in our work, home lives, and even personal space."
~Jane Beshear, former First Lady of Kentucky

"Lisa Miller has produced a gem that will empower women and help them live up to their fullest potential. The Heart of Leadership for Women: Cultivating a Sacred Space is a perfect template to blend the material and spiritual life. Lisa has not only studied but has applied all of these principles in her own transformation. Meditation and gratitude can be very powerful to maintain harmony in all areas of life."
~Dr. Suhas Kshirsagar BAMS, MD.; Ayurvedic physician and best selling author of *Change Your Schedule, Change Your Life*

"Lisa is an authentic leader who knows how to support people where they shine. Now more than ever, empowering women to develop and own their strengths is essential."
~Melissa Etheridge, rock icon and activist

The HEART of LEADERSHIP for Women

Cultivating a Sacred Space

Dear Karen,
It is so wonderful to be in
the Heart of this with you!
X Lisa

Lisa M. Miller

BALBOA.PRESS

A DIVISION OF HAY HOUSE

Balboa Press books may be ordered through booksellers or by contacting:

Balboa Press
A Division of Hay House
1663 Liberty Drive
Bloomington, IN 47403
www.balboapress.com
1 (877) 407-4847

Because of the dynamic nature of the Internet, any web addresses or links contained in this book may have changed since publication and may no longer be valid. The views expressed in this work are solely those of the author and do not necessarily reflect the views of the publisher, and the publisher hereby disclaims any responsibility for them.

The author of this book does not dispense medical advice or prescribe the use of any technique as a form of treatment for physical, emotional, or medical problems without the advice of a physician, either directly or indirectly. The intent of the author is only to offer information of a general nature to help you in your quest for emotional and spiritual well-being. In the event you use any of the information in this book for yourself, which is your constitutional right, the author and the publisher assume no responsibility for your actions.

Any people depicted in stock imagery provided by Getty Images are models, and such images are being used for illustrative purposes only. Certain stock imagery © Getty Images.

Print information available on the last page.

ISBN: 978-1-9822-4099-8 (sc)
ISBN: 978-1-9822-4101-8 (hc)
ISBN: 978-1-9822-4100-1 (e)

Library of Congress Control Number: 2020900442

Balboa Press rev. date: 02/18/2020

*To my beloved mentors of two decades who continue to guide me
through the heart of leadership:
Gene,
Rosalyn, and Ken,
J.P
May you receive tenfold the blessings you've gifted me and others.*

✻

*To R.T, Marnie, and Beth: Thank you dearly for
helping me gather and sow inspiration for this book
through sisterhood, ceremony, and great fun.*

*To Leslie and Pamela: Thank you for
encouraging me from the beginning.*

*To Kim and Fran: Thank you for your steadfast
unconditional love from the beginning of everything.*

To Dr. Suhas: Thank you for the timely confidence and resolve.

To Mariabruna: Thank you for the cheers and attentive support.

To Jonathan: Thank you for decades of love and partnership.

*Importantly, to the wonderful women of so many Circles:
Thank you for showing up year after year, theme after theme,
and for co-cultivating our transformative sacred spaces.*

✻

*To my reassuring and generous team of readers and editors: Rosalyn,
Mariabruna, Jonathan, Leslie, Rhonda, France, Jane, Dr. S, and Ron,
I'm deeply grateful.*

Contents

SECTION 4
Afterward and Afterword. The Garland. Evaluation. Begin Again.

Introduction

Elevate any event from a get-together to a sacred gathering. This book will show you how.

This is for every workshop and therapeutic-arts facilitator, retreat leader, instructor, artist and performer, studio owner, activist, speaker, event-coordinator, life coach, healer... and more. The potential for healing, no matter the context, is exponential when people gather for the purpose of self-exploration in personal health and the health of others, for the purpose of inspiration, and for right action toward community and global health.

And, if the gathering is set up with the objective of support, learning, and laughter, participants will inspire one another while exploring their own depth of personal potential and wisdom. There, the gathering will have become a sacred one.

If cultivating and holding a transformative space for others is strong in you, a space in which you can all blossom and move in the direction of healing and joy, you are a leader, and you're reading the right guide. Whether new to facilitation or seasoned, you will see that this book is overflowing with the h*eart* of cultivating a sacred space inherent in your leadership efforts.

Here, references to "space" are about so much more than physical location. The intention that supports the gathering *is* the very nourishment in the soil, it's the potential that is held for participants; the space we furnish with our knowledge, guidance, inclusion, and heart.

As a facilitator, if you happen to be prone to laughter and fun (and a bit of irreverence), those qualities will inevitably show up with you.

Either way, healing and growth are always a given—especially for you, the leader.

Truly, for the conscious facilitator planning a gathering designed to inspire and empower with roots in the grounding of teachings and history and art tried and true, there are greater forces at work than merely a plan for a get-together.

Anyone who's been educated in something can talk about what they've learned and facilitate it in the most basic ways by sharing information and experience—we do that all the time over coffee. But it's the *conscious, careful* group facilitator who elevates the communication of those teachings from basic, to something with more capacity for enduring healing impact.

For a person attracted to leadership in service, it's wonderfully exciting to think about facilitation as a way of being a conduit for wisdom, not only as a way to keep knowledge alive and to help mobilize change, but as a way for others to join in the responsibility of that, and to help expand conscious living as a therapeutic force in the world at large.

This is what Brother David Steindl-Rast,[1] a great inspirer of the gratitude movement calls Contemplation in Action: The way for the richness of life to flow through you.

This book is about finding your way and then stepping fully into your empowerment as a woman who shines a light for other women to find theirs, whatever your theme, whatever *their* paths. It's about bringing the sacred inherent in leadership into your gathering space and making it visible and accessible for your attendees; it's about *holding* the sacred space for others once it's been cultivated in the weeks, sometimes years of your preparation.

Once you do that, participants can take it from there: Access their individual sacred interior worlds and gather volition and momentum to deepen intuition, health, and the contribution to community.

---

[1] www.Gratefullness.org

As an intentional sacred space cultivator and discerning student myself, I'll share exactly what has worked out well and not so well for me over 20 years of leadership, from community activism, teaching and speaking, to facilitating in one-on-one therapeutic settings.

Along with my early career training as a Summer Camp Director, as a Family Systems Therapy researcher, as a clinical chaplain, and through the non-profit I founded, my most focused work and credentials in a variety of healing modalities have provided me rich facilitation experience. They include: Indigenous energy healing, Mussar Group Facilitation, Meditation, Yoga, Ayurvedic Health Coaching, and, SoulCollage® Facilitation.

For years, I grew into leadership while my husband held elected office. I will tell you that even for the spouse, public office leadership requires some big time equilibrium finesse and a willingness to lean into personal correction, accountability, and the evolution of grace.

Today still, I'm in love with creating a sacred space for women to learn and grow through workshops, retreats, and support groups. What one woman shares about her experience can unexpectedly ignite a profound realization for another. The healing contagion grows. And magic happens.

Divine intervention.

But because my belief in myself as a leader was once only as high as a mushroom (and probably only the stem), I know that the missteps, bruises and doubts, were perhaps more valuable than the easy wins; they provided the most insight for growth. For me, they were most certainly the shitty (!) vital fertilizer to the flowering magnolia tree that I am today. I'm grateful for all of it.

And if I can do it, you can.

Here, though I write with a feminine voice to newer female leaders, I hope readers of every ilk and level of experience find benefit in these pages—some little gems to shine along the path forward. After all, we all exist with some inner feminine spirit just as we do masculine. And every leader I know benefits from beginner's mind—that delicious state of openness to fresh perspective, and availability, to the present moment.

The he*art* of leadership and the cultivation of the sacred space therein, is truly for everyone.

If something inside you feels like YES as you read this, you have every reason to know that you are a leader. Now, continue to be one who helps others grow into their potential as you grow throughout your lifetime, fully into yours.

Join me as we play in the inspired context of the Women's Circle.

As always, I'm looking forward to being there with you.

A hug,
Lisa

Preface

Why Women Come Together. And Why Doing So Creates Dynamic Potential

Sometimes workshop participants decide to attend an advertised event because the theme sparked a little interest, or maybe it hit right on, but rarely is a first-timer aware that by showing up, she is actually bringing a wealth of deep knowing, wisdom, and inner Light for the benefit of every other woman in the gathering. That she is bringing her team of angels and guides in spirit, and *their* wisdom for everyone in attendance.

A first-timer probably isn't aware that she holds a wealth of vital wisdom and experience, at all. Or that she can tap into it anytime and all the time—live from it—that it is a reliable source of powerful intuition. That she doesn't have to constantly try to grasp for answers outside herself from Gurus (or leaders!) of all sorts.

Likely, the newcomer is hardly aware that *her* spiritual "team" of angels and guides and resonant archetypes have been trying to communicate with her for some time—through all of her life challenges and celebrations—trying to say:

Dear one, look this way, here is a resource—a little symbol, event, book, synchronicity—that represents the answer to the prayer you've been whispering all this time.

And imagine how powerful is the workshop or retreat for the returning participant who knows what to expect, is excited and open to it, and might even long for it. Who becomes a part of the retreat's healing, beauty, and power.

More than handfuls of times, participants share the following sentiment articulated brilliantly by one frequent attendee:

"The Women's Circle introduces me to myself. Every time."

It is the group energy (full of newcomers and returning participants combined) that helps every woman open to what has been inside her and around her all along.

For every participant and facilitator alike, the sacred space inherent in the gathering is nothing short of miraculous. And it is not out of the ordinary. Nor relegated to a certain holy time, or place, or "evolved" people. It is for everyone, all the time, and in any location where people with an open heart are interested in self-exploration.

Even though we live vastly different lives, what we all share is the physical, emotional, mental, and spiritual understanding of personhood and womanhood. And how life is. And how it can be. And how much we all pray for love, and satisfaction, and peace, and joy. And maybe sisterhood, now too.

And then, when it's over, whether it's been a 90 minute gathering, several hours together, or a weekend-long retreat or training, participants have gained new tools and new excitement for moving forward in some small way, or profound. This is the beauty, magic, and power of a women's gathering.

And simply, it's just really great fun. All natural. The side effects include balance and more joy for daily life.

And sisterhood, of course.

Beginning

Seeding Goals:

This is a space that's dreamy, hopeful, heart-full, spiritual. Pregnant with potential.

Chapter 1

It Begins With Gratitude and Meditation. Oh Yah

As temporary, fragile and vulnerable our bodies are, they
are most direct portals to the only forever there is.

~Geneen Roth

Be. Then, Do

Your desire to lead is a calling.

As a leader, it's how you dwell in your preparation hours, in the facilitation hours, and in the after hours of your event, that makes your leadership a sacred experience for you and others.

Facilitating a gathering of some sort is about the service of others, but this sacred work is also about you. Leadership inevitably connects you to something bigger: God, Universe, Spirit, non-local intelligence, life—whatever name and face of that something bigger with which you identify.

In service as a leader, you are meant to grow and benefit too, sometimes even first, so that you can fill yourself up enough to give from the overflow.

In your overflow will be the thrill of your learning and education, your passion to pass it on, your self-care momentum, and your connection to the-something-bigger of life. And simply but compellingly, the wisdom you've gained from your decades of life experience.

That is *live it to give it* influence. Sacred *living it.*

When all of that conscious awareness and edification are your strategy for leadership, what you want for your attendees will effortlessly emerge and expand in ways you can't predict they even need. It will be something wonderful beyond your imagining. And you will have been a helpful catalyst of it. Giving from the overflow allows you to give without burning out from the giving, and to benefit *through* the process itself.

Naturally, by meeting the sacred in and around yourself first, you carry the potential for others.

This type of leadership is less about doing something, or bringing something, or making something happen, than it is about *being* something: a conscious, confident, skilled, joyful, prepared facilitator.

It's about being a grateful one. Daily.

A Dose of Daily Gratitude Since Antiquity: The Map AND the Navigation Tool

> *A low prayer, a high prayer, I send through space.*
> *Arrange them Thyself, O King of Grace* [2]

Among people across the globe over eons of time, gratitude rituals, actions, and even impish Gaelic poetry have given thanks while elevating the human spirit. Gratitude becomes us, human species that we are. It's a shining virtue that leads the way, and even miraculous in nature as it sets the tone for feelings, beliefs, behaviors and, in a professional context, one's perspective concerning goals and the approach to them.

---

[2] Eleanor Hull, The Poem-Book of Gael: Translations from Irish-Gaelic Poetry into English Prose and Verse (Adamant Media, London).

And, there is another merit inherent in gratitude that serves humanity: Gratitude leads to *life meaning*. We're meant to use what we find there—at the intersection between self and the external world—and to grow and make more meaning of it all for everyday living.

This is why a daily gratitude practice is one small but significant way toward being an effective leader. It's a contagious energy; not only does embodying it make meaning grow concerning everything in your life, it helps others to grow awareness of the inherent meaning in theirs.

The Solid Ground Beneath Their Dancing Feet

When you as a leader can personify this energy, not just tap it for a moment here and there but really live from it, it sets up your facilitation space no matter where you locate your physical space. The effect: Gratitude is enlivened as a vital nutrient in the soil of what you're cultivating.

Simply, it gets the good-retreat-momentum-ball rolling for you.

What's more, your attendees want to feel your gratitude and excitement integrated into the invitation to join your event (and if you feel joy and awe, that's really good too, it'll make the invitation more compelling). Those integral elements become the foundation of your event because they're the bedrock that will support your attendees when they arrive, and will help them to relax even though they may not consciously know why it feels so good to step into the energy of the space that you've set up for their benefit.

Cicero said so: "Gratitude is not only the greatest of virtues, but the parent of all the others."

As a first timer, an attendee might not know what "energy of the space" even means. But don't we all appreciate something solid beneath our dancing feet, and our resting bodies, even if we don't know what that solidity is made of?

I have found this to be true again and again and again through the years in my most successful gatherings.

Affects and Effects of the Gratitude Meditation Cocktail

Gratitude when mixed with meditation or a contemplative practice is potent: Prevailing wisdom from ancient masters have extoled the advantage of a daily meditation routine.

There, I said it again: *Daily.*

Like the necessity of eating, the nourishment of meditation (with gratitude) must also be dosed into daily fulfillment in order that it serve you effectively, and serve others positively.

Masters explain that in so doing, the deeper aspect of self—the human spirit beyond the ego connected to the conscious intelligence of the Universe—can become active enough to direct one's life choices. Here's Father Richard Rohr in his newsletter from the The Center for Action and Contemplation:

"Silence needs to be understood in a larger way than simply a lack of audible noise. Whenever emptiness—what seems like empty space or absence of sound—becomes its own kind of fullness with its own kind of sweet voice, we have just experienced sacred silence."[3]

When you're aligned with that big wisdom, even your impulses will lead to unexpected gains and meaningful coincidences. For example, though you normally go straight home after work on Tuesdays, you follow an impulse to stop at a bakery on the way. There, you find yourself in line overhearing a detailed endorsement about a venue you're considering for your next event.

---

[3] Father Richard Rohr: Newsletter from the The Center for Action and Contemplation, January 9, 2020

The spiritual explanation of the potency of meditation teaches that the silent spaces between thoughts—the most sought after effects of quieting the monkey mind—are exactly the spaces in which the soul abides. Quieting the endless chatter gives one's soul more "space" to exist in a human experiential life. Gives it volume. Gives you the capacity to hear its direction toward the fulfillment of your desires.

And, modern scientific explanation behind the dynamism of a daily meditation practice is this:

Quieting the mind rewires the primitive human fight-flight reactivity of the central nervous system; turns *down* the perception of stressors at every turn and corner, and straight line.

Even mere moments of silence in the space between thoughts, is deeply, neurologically and physically healing. Just as any muscle becomes stronger through practice, a meditation habit teaches the body to bypass the primeval brain "reactivity" of the amygdala (think cave man survival), to allow instead an ability to "respond" from higher wisdom faculties no matter how intense the stressor (think Nelson Mandela survival).

A restful responsive relationship with one's environment and the world at large not only allows an admirable level of serenity and peace, but along with that central nervous system "rewiring" is optimal immune function, lower blood pressure, great creativity, and a pervasive feeling of *I got this*-ness.

Restful responsiveness ushers in a more balanced relationship with self.

Gratitude, and a meditative practice of some sort are the secret weapons of successful, stable, dynamic leaders. You can receive the very same professional certification training as the next woman; what can set you apart is *your* elevated spirit to create something special for your participants by being grounded and confident, open to Spirit's influence, and, sincerely grateful for your life—whatever your path has been.

Without a doubt, as a facilitator, you've truly got it goin' on when your leadership style is guided by your higher acumen and deeper wisdom.

But clearing some internal space in order to sense this guidance might be first in order.

(This is not about competition, by the way. Rather, it's about knowing that *your* leadership abilities are strong based on authentic grounded-ness, which in turn can give *you* the confidence you need to move forward and *not* compare yourself to others. There are enough leadership styles on the planet to satisfy every need, you and your attendees included. There *are* people looking for your innate gifts and what you have to offer! It'll be much easier for y'all to find one another when between you, you're more confident.)

Meditation is not just the arena of modern Gurus like Tich Naht Hanh, Pema Chodron, Tara Brach, but popular-culture role models too: Ellen DeGeneres, Clint Eastwood, Russel Brand, and, Kobe Bryant. In an Oprah.com video (visit YouTube: Kobe on Oprah, Meditation Dictates My Day), Bryant offered that his morning meditation practice is like an anchor for the day that allows him to be "set" for whatever might come. Have you seen him on the basketball court? He goes with the flow, man.

More relevant here: Meditation is also the arena of the humble multitudes around the globe who less visibly but effectively help their communities heal and grow.

It is also your arena.

When the Answer was: "Meditation Lisa"

If you are reading this recruitment to begin or deepen a meditation and gratitude practice, and you're feeling some internal resistance, know that I have been there my friend. In 2005 I went into my first meditation retreat with some hope, and left with great irritation. And resentment.

I wanted the promised benefits: The meditation-after-glow, the Zen-like disposition, the optimal blood pressure icing on the meditation cake. But I looked at my watch every two to three minutes of the 30 minute practice, and faked an asthma attack to have an excuse to leave the room half way through..

However, I was told that it would merely take a little time and "practice" to achieve the payoff including decreased anxiety, increased creativity and vitality, and patience. And all that stuff about decreased cortisol output and less sticky blood platelets—I wanted that too. When I looked at others who paid homage to meditation (Oprah!), I felt I could at least try it for the prescribed minimum-21-day-essential-habit-forming-effort.

(And I could quit on day 22, if it hadn't worked.)

At home, around day 15 of my new dedicated meditation (irritation) practice, something happened. My handyman, a big middle aged guy whose name we'll say is Allen, was installing a fan in my attic when he fell half-way through the attic floor—which was also the vaulted ceiling of my living room. As he held on by the armpits, the closet floor was 20 feet below. There was falling drywall, kicking dangling legs, and, screaming (his, not mine). I saw, heard, and felt, the whole thing. All of it. His terror was remarkable.

But my reaction to near disaster? Apparently, it was a response from the state of *restful awareness* that Deepak Chopra himself had promised during my recent meditation retreat for both mundane and challenging stressors:

> "Allen, it's okay, it's gonna be okay. Take a breath and
> pull yourself back up. You can do it. It's okay. When you
> come downstairs, I'll get you some water."

The kicking and screaming stopped, he managed to pull himself back up and made it down from the attic in one piece. And then on quivering legs (his, not mine), I escorted him to a kitchen chair

Later that night, in the aftermath, when I looked at the big, big-man sized tear in my hallway ceiling, I thought to myself:

Who was that calm, cool superwoman who averted human disaster? Ohhhh, THAT was Meditation Lisa.

Six years later in 2011, I became a Meditation Instructor through the Chopra Center for Wellbeing, and have been relying on my gratitude-meditation-combo superwoman-power tool, ever since—especially in my professional life where there can be a lot less predictability and more room for things to fall through (Ha! See what I did there?).

Since meditating with gratitude nearly every day in recent years, all my relationships have improved, including the one with myself—my soul. I can more easily hear and feel its direction. As an extension, my relationship with God has evolved and deepened too.

What's more, the retreats I facilitate now are rich for many women in attendance because I hold the space more effectively and can truly go with the flow. My disposition holds more bandwidth. In my professional relationships, I'm the first beneficiary of this affect effect.

I'm the Kobe Bryant of the retreat space.

How to Personify It: Taking Gratitude and Meditation Out of Your Head and into Your Aura

For gratitude and the calming wisdom effects of meditation to truly take root, be grooved into you, they must be embodied. You can't just think about them and how important they are—you must *feel* them.

From the Stress Reduction Clinic of Jon Kabat-Zin, to Jack Kornfield's Meditation for Beginners videos and books, to Deepak and Oprah's 21 Day Meditation Challenge, to Andy Puddicombe's HeadSpace app, and more (!), there are many accessible ways to learn how to sit in silence, rewire your hypervigilant-reactive-instincts, and quiet your mind enough to feel the presence and wisdom of your own soul.

No matter which gratitude and meditation practice you choose, I want to suggest a preface of five essential soul questions to precede meditation, that have helped to enhance my life both personally and professionally.

Based on centuries-old wisdom about meditation and a life of balance, Dr. Deepak taught and reinforced these five questions in my first meditation retreat, and in the hundreds of hours of classes and training in his certification programs—Meditation, and Ayurveda, respectively. Here's his direction; I'll paraphrase (insert soothing Indian accent):

Before you focus your mind into silence, drop these questions like pebbles into the stream of consciousness that is your being. It's not the answering of the questions that is important; it's the questions themselves that will connect you more intimately with your life and with your purpose in this life. We ask the questions before silence so that they can become anchored into consciousness. So that we find ourselves living the answers.

Who am I? What do I want? What is my purpose? How can I serve? For what am I grateful?

I can't say enough about how the essential nature of these questions have helped me especially on days when getting out of bed and doing grown-up things feels challenging. The point about asking the questions to live out the answers… Turns out, that's completely true—they have become embedded in both my unconscious motives and my conscious ones. Those simple questions have buoyed me when I've needed it most.

As a facilitator, others are looking to you as a resource and a leader. How and who you are in some contexts, even when no one is looking, is how and who you have the capacity to be in others. Living what you want to teach is the only way to make your teachings integrate-able for others. You can only take your students as far as you have been, and can sustain, yourself.

Early *Meditation Lisa* is the poster child for the truth that what happens during your meditation practice (cough cough) (irritation irritation) is not important; it's what your meditation *effort* allows to happen in the remaining hours of the day. Consistently, even brief moments of stillness can yield phenomenal gains.

Today, I also emulate Abraham-Hicks general direction:

Just 15 or 20 minutes a day. Focus on a boring noise in your room, like the hum of the air conditioner, to allow your mind a break from thinking in order to reset your alignment with Source.

Your personal energy of self-care and how you live your life is a language all its own when you're leading. And it's louder than the words you speak. You carry it in with you when you step into the room. If the virtue of gratitude gets the ball rolling for your event preparation and then supports your participants in the sacred space you've created, your stability and endurance while with them is dependent on the wise, "restful awareness" of your higher nature.

Before every event you lead, go deep into the Thank Yous—it's a most reliable tool for shaping the beautiful thing you're planning. And then silence your busy mind so that you can receive the insights and inspirations ready to be known *through* you.

Wisdom traditions around the world have put gratitude and meditation squarely on the map of human-journey navigation; the terrain may change over millennia, but those tools grow in strength through the stories of intrepid travelers who confirm the path.

Chapter 2

Seeds, Ritual, Delight

Isn't it wonderful to discover that you are the one you've been waiting for? That you truly are the love of your life!

~Byron Katie

An Idea Seeds Journal is Not Just for Literate Birds

O nce gratitude is your fertile soil, your dreams have a place to land and germinate. Intention grows from your dreams and cultivates the structure of your gathering in ways you can't predict or imagine will be beautiful, and useful, for those who attend your event.

To figure out the ins and outs of your potential plans, and to capture the brilliant ideas whirling through the ether awaiting your attention and use (that's right, it's all right there for you to pluck), here's some pragmatic focus:

I suggest finding a lovely notebook you're attracted to. It'll be your Idea Seeds Journal for the events you plan in the coming year. Using it will become a ritual you come back to time and time again when daydreaming your plans into reality. Rituals, even little ones like this gain a momentum that helps in the continuing progress and expansion of your goals. Legal note pads are fine for some things, but why begin with "fine" when something like "lovely" is another option? Do you want *fine* or do you want *lovely* for your event?

Here's why there's a difference, and why you should consider something (seemingly trivial) like the use of a journal/notebook as an important tool in the making of your dreams and goals:

1) Unlike legal pads without covers, a journal/notebook has two— front and back. Covers are symbolic for holding space for your thoughts, questions, ideas, and all your research in between.

   A journal/notebook has a spine. Like your physical body, the purpose of the book structure is given to holding the heart of everything it contains; all the seeds of your project.

   Think of your journal as a tool that you use to fashion your finished product; not only does it maintain its contents in an organized and protective way, if it's visually pleasing to notice on your work table, you'll be drawn to it. Essentially, it's a symbolic tool that will enhance your effort in creating something beautiful. When your tools are pleasing to work with, you *want* to work with them. That *wanting*, supports your goal.

2) A journal/notebook can be used continuously for the planning of many gatherings in your future. Among all your other office notebooks, it's easily identifiable as the one used for planning; the seed planting of your events.

   Even after the first event, your designated Idea Seeds Journal will be the container for the breadth of your creativity. It will become a sacred container of daydreams, research, action steps, and will help you gain momentum through the practice of planning and facilitating. Eventually, your journals will hold your leadership and facilitation history; history will propel you forward.

3) Most importantly, if you have the notion that you're on your own in creating something, let me help you here:

Girlfriend, there's a whole team on your team. Hopefully you're feeling them a little more now that you're meditating. And gratitude-ing.

Especially through your heart for service, your Spirit Guides want to help you. A dedicated journal/notebook is both a tangible and and energetic way to open to Spirit and the inspiration ready to be communicated to you. Your Idea Seeds Journal is the very place for holy ideas to happen. And that's helpful in order for *the sacred* of life to find an easy path straight to your door.

Moreover, immediately following your gratitude and meditation practice, when you open your dedicated journal and sit down with it, it's a signal to your Spirit Guides that *you* are open to inspiration. Sitting with a pen and blank page is your gesture for openness to receiving. It's a ritual that can propel you into the state of mind and heart toward your goal.

It will enhance the invitation for brilliant ideas to come sit *with* you.

Simple, ordinary things call the sacred to you and enhance your delight in them.

On a final note, and speaking pragmatically again, Higher Power is always looking for a way to get through to you. It's much easier for your etheric helpers when you're in a reliably organized receiving mode and just simply delighted about something you believe is trivial, like the lovely little Journal you've designated for the job.

Delight is delight, it captures the Light!

Chapter 3

Leadership: Sometimes You Feel Called, Sometimes You Call, Know When to Change Direction

The place God calls you to is the place where your deep gladness and the world's deep hunger meet.

~Frederick Buechner

You've felt moved to lead, facilitate, teach, or guide others in some way. Maybe your inspiration has come from your own personal learning and interests, or your light-hearted desire to be of service, or your professional certified training. Or maybe, it's something else. Like a pressing need in your community, or country, or world as a whole that compels you to take action from deep in your soul.

Whatever the ignition of the present spark in you, light or deep—your conscious awareness of *what* and *why* are important. Acknowledging the answers to these vital questions will inform your decisions and will keep you focused in your call to leadership, from the genesis of that call.

Essentially, this awareness will help you to keep going on days when you are tired. It will help you know when the time is right to begin. And just as important, your conscious awareness of the *what* and *why* of your leadership will help you know when and if, it is time to stop.

Or at least change direction.

Years ago, with my husband Jonathan, we had to bring that conscious awareness to our dedicated life in politics. To begin it. And eventually, to leave it.

In 1997, by age 30, when we were new parents to babies ages one and three, Jonathan had held numerous senior positions in federal government already. When we moved "back home" to Kentucky from Washington D.C, he felt called to step front and center into political leadership. It had been building in his bones since adolescence, and while looking at the needs of his home state through skilled educated eyes, he "called" that responsibility even closer. As a father, his intentions for creating programs to help Kentucky families became specific. He felt compelled.

So that's what we set our intentions upon and moved forward from there.

A year after an unsuccessful first bid for Congress in 1998, we ran for State Treasurer and won. Jonathan was elected to that office twice (1999, 2003) and served for eight years in our state capitol. As that service headed toward conclusion we campaigned for Governor (2007), unsuccessfully. I had my own platform by that time as the founder and CEO of Girls Rock!, a self-esteem and empowerment program for girls and their mothers. So despite our disappointment, still, he kept on; there were plenty of other leadership needs in our state.

After several more years in politics—working in the Governor's cabinet and leading the Kentucky Democratic Party—it became clear to Jonathan that it was time to change career direction. By our mid 40's, decades of political leadership had been enough. We knew we were no longer happy and excited about standing front and center in the political arena. We could feel in our souls that we had done justice to the original calling, offered what we could, and that it was time not just to "leave politics," but to make room for others to step in.

Importantly, as a couple—as a family—we were all tired and we knew it. Burned-out with a capitol B. A political life, the campaign life of loosing some, winning some, is intensely taxing. Our kids were teenagers. They needed a Dad who would be more present, and we needed to re-evaluate ourselves as a couple.

And thank goodness we were awake to those deep acknowledgements. It was a crucial conscious knowing that would shape the following years of our lives.

It's easy to continue doing something just because it's always been the way to do things. As a leader, knowing when to reassess, when to stop, when to move in a different direction, is crucial to personal emotional and spiritual fulfillment, and to physical health.

The clue that it's time for re-evaluation? The original call feels silent in your heart.

I'll confide, at times, the idea of "quitting" was an excruciating one: To leave the thing that our lifestyle was tied to—Jonathan's identity was tied to it—to rethink our purpose related to social justice specifically, was very hard to come to terms with. My husband had grown up believing deeply in political leadership; he was the two-year-old who could recite all the presidents in order. And no kidding: backwards.

What helped during that re-evaluation time was a glimmer of knowing that there would be another way to serve through a leadership role. Another doorway. We didn't know what or how it would be, but we knew with patience and time it would become clear for him and our family— another imperative vocation—other fulfilling and contributing roles.

There's always at least a glimmer of clarity. Our human task is to stay awake and open enough to recognize the glimmer and to explore the direction it illuminates.

(And that is exactly what happened for Jonathan—for us. After a recovery period, he found that outside of political office he could more effectively create exciting new bi-partisan programs for Kentucky and our country. Turns out that he'd honed his skills in diplomacy on the job all those years. Not only were his new programs effective, but beyond the purview of bureaucratic red tape, they were and are great fun to work on. He loves his work years later, today. And as a result, I'll confide that we're happier than we've ever been as a family.)

Your personal awareness, staying conscious of the why you want to facilitate or contribute to anything in any way, endows your leadership with purpose, and with drive, and with a sense of the sacred that enlivens it. This is vital. Being conscious of your *why* will make your heart sing and will help you up get up in the morning to go do it. And when you no longer feel it in your heart, your original conscious awareness will help you notice its absence—the big signal that something is off—that you need help, or significant change.

As you move toward your call to leadership, it will serve you well to know now that when and if you no longer feel aligned with the genesis of the calling, it may mean that you have done all you could do.

Or maybe an exciting enhancement awaits you. Metamorphosis.

When the Call to Leadership Bangs on Your Door

Sometimes you feel specifically *called* in a very specific, specific way. Let me reinforce this with something specific:

In 2004, before I had a desire to teach and lead the way I do now, the question: *what is your unique passion in service?* was a faint voice. I was a full time mother focused on raising my seven and nine year-old daughters in the midst of Jonathan's political career demands. Often, I felt I was treading water just to keep our family's life in order. And trying to get enough sleep.

But because of my consuming commitment to raising emotionally and physically healthy daughters, something happened that burst that question about passion into the reality of my family life. It happened when my nine year-old, in the fourth grade, announced on a Friday afternoon that she "would not eat this weekend because the girls at school want to be skinny."

Because I had carefully set up a home environment characterized by non-judgment (had banned diet conversation among my extended family in our ear shot), I knew my daughter's announcement was less about her view of herself at the time and more about the effect of her peers and our culture on her emerging identity. It was about a world of overwhelming media messages and pervasive narrow standards of beauty for girls and women. In North America, it seemed not much had changed since my own childhood.

But in the moment of "not eating this weekend," what I *knew* was irrelevant. All I felt was desperation.

Fear. And hopelessness. If I couldn't protect my kid what could I possibly do about anything?

That question was a turning point.

By the end of the weekend, I felt the stirrings of something else. Resolve. Inspiration. Passion. Commitment to helping find a solution, and to help make that solution a reality.

Like my mother, aunts, cousins and grandmothers, I too had struggled with an overly critical internal voice about physical appearance. Though I knew I couldn't erase ubiquitous cultural biases, from my new rage and mother-bear motivation came hope that I could in fact provide some kind of antidote for us all. I knew there had to be a solution that could serve not just my own girls, but all the daughters in their school, and the young helpless internal girl inside myself. Intuitively, I knew that the mothers of girls in my town needed a way to truly let *themselves* off the "hot" body hook.

The solution for my daughter needed to be a comprehensive one.

Feeling compelled to take action—step into a visible facilitative role—I called our family pediatrician, the incomparable Dr. Hood (who would become an enduring champion force behind the productive actions I would take). Her immediate encouragement propelled me forward, and together, we talked about the essential emotional esteem needed for girls to grow up healthfully. In the first of many conversations we would have over the years, we envisioned mothers teaching their girls how to love themselves while we learned to teach our own.

So, with moral support and a volunteer commitment from health professionals and facilitating teens in my city, it was just weeks before founding *Girls Rock! Workshops for Girls and Moms*, a healthy body-image and self-esteem program. Our first workshop a great success with14 attending moms and girls, ten facilitating professionals, and seven teen mentors. It was a resource that we could all lean on.

I would say that I felt less called, and more *driven*, toward the solution that Girls Rock! and the resources it would provide. It was most definitely an urgent, banging-on-my-door call to leadership. I didn't know ahead of time I was prepared to take it on. But as solutions fell into place so swiftly—service professionals kept saying yes to helping—every indication about timing clearly said: NOW.

Girls Rock! Inc. facilitated workshops annually for many years. We became a non-profit with 100 people in attendance at times. The teen mentors of the program and I, wrote a book:

Girls Rock! Just the Way We Are. Published in 2005, it was read all over North America until it's final printing in 2017.

Once the program was born, from my initial drive for a solution and the first small but powerful workshop gathering, for the duration of its life until 2017, Girls Rock! was among the only organized public self-esteem resource for girls in my state. In addition to coordinating our mom/daughter workshops and our book, I spoke at all kinds of conferences in Kentucky and beyond with my team of teen mentors. For 13 years, I was recruited to speak at education meetings, the Health Department, and at local schools.

From my initial very personal (problem based) drive, my sustained driving passion evolved and solidified: For my daughters to grow up in a community that would embrace diversity, and to educate and provide this diversity resource where needed, in my region and beyond. The solution that Girls Rock! provided my family and community gained a momentum all its own, which effectively kept me going—running it.

Feeling It, and Then Afterward

The service your leadership provides others should also feed you.

Aside from the direct feedback received, that Girls Rock! offered something of value to attendees, how did *I* know I was doing the right thing?

I *felt* it. I felt fulfilled while doing all of it.

For me, continuing to run and grow Girls Rock! programming felt exciting, and hopeful, and pressing, compelling, and full of potential and new opportunities. I thought about it and designed program and book features while going about the mundane details of my day, and especially when I thought about my girls' futures. I mulled over details before I went to sleep at night and when I woke up in the morning. When I talked about Girls Rock! with my daughters and family, and the teams of mentors and volunteers, I felt my heart swell. It became a part of my heart and my purpose to the contribution of a healthier culture—even just the little bit I could influence. And next to raising my daughters it felt like my life's work. I finally understood from a deeper place how my husband felt about his.

The more fulfilled you are in service, the better your service.

Then, after 13 years, when my girls were young women (and after they'd become Girls Rock! mentors themselves) though I wasn't burned-out, I no longer felt fulfilled through the Girls Rock! contribution. Nor essential. Recognizing the absence of those feelings in my leadership role was key, because absence was again an essential guidepost.

What's more, I realized that my heart and gut had gotten what they needed in satisfying exchange for that particular leadership role, for more than a decade. I got just as much out of leadership as I had offered. There might be other callings eventually. Other ways I could feel fulfilled and passionate while contributing in service.

Importantly, by the time I retired the program, more self-esteem curricula had found roots in my city—I knew I could retire Girls Rock! Inc. not just because I wanted and needed to, but because there were others who were carrying on with the work of empowering girls.

Not Reinventing the Wheel, And, Timing

You do not have to run for political office or give birth to a non-profit organization in order to allow the full blossoming of your passion and drive. But you should recognize that if you feel an urgency or joy of some sort about facilitating something, or performing, or organizing, or writing or making art that shines more Light into this world we live in, you *are* feeling passion about that topic and its partnered action for some good reason. Explore the why and what. But then determine carefully if your life is resonant to facilitate that urgency. Just because you feel called, does not mean you must answer with action immediately the way I did with the creation of Girls Rock!.

It could be a slow climb, as Jonathan's was.

In any case, your decision to pick up leadership and facilitation should feel like a process of co-creation, not pressure. Lean on *your* training and experience, whatever that is. Seek more of it if you need to. That was key for me, with Girls Rock! I sought out local and regional experts and enrolled in training, and found national curricula with proven efficacy. Educators, performers and artists learn and then practice. Preparation is as essential as showing up.

I want to point out here that where my "education" was lacking in the area of programming and running a non-profit, I asked for help from experts and educated myself and sought some training. I did not wait to earn additional degrees before feeling worthy of a new leadership role.

Wherever you are, *is* your point of entry. But I want to suggest that you enter and carry responsibility with at least some guidance and support.

As well, I want to stress the following: If you feel called to leadership among a population that is despairing, your call should feel sweetly resonant in the core of your being. Service should never be about sacrifice, nor pity, or a sense of rescuing duty. Rather, service in leadership should be about alignment with your purpose, your unique gifts, and your skills, so that you have something to serve *with*. Indeed, your self-care and conscious awareness is exactly where God is.

I would say that among a despairing population, it is vital that you feel a great resounding resonance in the core of your being because burn out happens swiftly there. Especially among those who carry a mantel without preparation and resources.

No matter the population you serve, your heartfelt sweet spot for them will carry your own self forward too.

If the opportunity is right, you'll feeeeeel it. And you should sleep on it. Take your time, if you can.

When Passion Is a Wee Voice

So maybe you're feeling called to something that meets the world's needs—or at least your community's, or at least among your friends and family—but you wouldn't classify that feeling as *passion* because you believe that passion has to feel big, and fiery, or compelling in the way I described my personal opening into leadership and facilitation.

But the truth is that big feelings are not the only calling into vital leadership. It's possible that your passion has been whispering to you over and over, for months or years, popping into your sensibility during mundane undertakings, trying to capture your attention.

If you give yourself space, give your soul and Higher Power the space and the opportunity to speak to you about its current focus, and longings, and joy, and confidence about what you need and what is needed in the world around you, What Do They Say???

So, But, And, Again, in order to hear that subtle voice, you must allow silence, and the weight of your soul, to take up some space in your life among your busy external environment, and your noisy inner one. And second. And third. And fourth.

Is there enough time and space in your day or week for this meeting with your own soul?

If so, do you need a little more patience to *allow* the fullness of that wisdom to speak up—break through the chaos of normal life-living habits and a noisy mind?

How's your 15-20 minute-daily-gratitude-meditation-practice going?

The answers to the soulful questions of your practice want to show up and answer you:

Who am I? What do I want? What is my purpose? How can I serve? For what am I grateful?

Maybe they are answering, have you noticed?

You Feel Needed, for Which Population?

However you look at quieter motivations, if you feel inspired around a certain topic, Life is choosing *you* to at least consider leadership. You might truly fill a need among other human beings in your town who would benefit from what you are moved to offer.

Even in the days of Girls Rock! coordinating, when my focus was mainly upon tween girls' curriculum, I was aware of a little pull toward wanting to help heal the grown women in attendance. G.R! led me to that. It wasn't a big light-bulb calling, it was a little pull at first. Today, from that long-ago quieter motivation, facilitating women's healing programming is the work I look forward to most. I love this work with this population more than any I've ever facilitated.

From working as a government official, Jonathan is now a bi-partisan liaison between government and its agencies, and all kinds of organizations and programs that serve citizen needs locally and nationally. Everything he has done, in all the ways he's served, has led him to his sweet-spot population today.

Which population lights up as your sweet spot? From among the general population you most identify with and like to spend time with, there might be a subset of people for whom your effort will be appropriate and most needed—people who will benefit from even more specialized facilitation that you can offer.

In the Girls Rock! years, I learned as I went along. Later, as I upgraded my skills and became certified in a variety of mind-body health modalities, and trained in chaplaincy, I became qualified to work with more intensive subjects.

Allow your gut, heart, and head—together with the voice of your soul's wisdom—to continue to communicate to your logical brain about the next best direction for your focus and action. Then, you'll be moving into something meaningful for your life in service—into creating and holding a sacred space for yourself and others, for the greater good.

If you're willing to do the leg work (with gratitude, meditation) that exists *at first* alongside your desire to facilitate, it'll become clear to you where you're best suited for leadership in the present chapter of your life. There might be more chapters later. But *right now* is all that's relevant. Once you listen to the small voice in your spirit that says *I could do that*, and notice that it feels like a YES in your gut and heart, your head can follow and begin to explore the possibilities.

Update your skills and practice your craft, or get educated, certified, or trained to facilitate something you're drawn to. And it can all get rolling.

Sometimes, you don't even have to dream very hard to find yourself in a position of facilitating because you will be led by the hand to a population that needs you. You will find yourself among them with some expertise to share. Even if it's not your "ideal" population or setting, it's the one that has emerged for your benefit, and theirs, right now. And it's ripe with practice opportunity and fine-tuning, and fun-tuning.

Remember, you're not doing it all alone. In the moments you feel some genuine inclination toward Tikkun Olam—making this world a better place, toward helping to relieve suffering and chaos of any sort—toward fulfilling a desire from the center of your being, the help that you need in order to be helpful is also assembling for you. You'll see and feel it along the way: people, resources, venues. Great Spirit.

Leadership, especially when it's full of gratitude, is a party!

Chapter 4

Questioning Who, What When

Everything you want is out there waiting for you to ask. Everything you want also wants you back. But you have to take action to get it.

~Jack Canfield

With Whom I don't know, I Just Feel I'm Supposed to Do Something

Again, it's in your capacity and influence to determine where it is that you fit in—where you can offer the best of your skills and time, and heart for giving. This is when meditating (and then journaling the answers) with some additional questions will be essential.

Call them Target-Population Meditations if you want:

Who do I most love to spend time with? In what settings am I most comfortable? In which contexts can I see myself as a leader? When I imagine myself among my target population, what am I doing? And who are the first faces that pop up when I imagine myself facilitating?

When you sit with these questions, it will help to have your Idea Seeds Journal handy. Writing allows you to explore your feeling state, and your feeling state will guide you. Here's an old entry of mine, on the topic of what I wanted to bring into a new retreat space with women:

Leadership in its best form: *Clear intention, followed by action, based in the spirit of human growth—soul growth. Service to humanity. Community awareness. Delight. Professionalism, care and thoughtfulness. The language of story. The language of hope, survival and empowerment. The hero's journey (read more on this—Joseph Campbell). Making meaning from hardship. No human is "alone" in her pain. Re read* Anatomy of the Spirit[4]. *Need to continue to explore this. Will talk to JP.*

Notice how my musings started off in a general direction—leadership, love, humanity—and became specific near the end to embrace language of story, language of hope, the realization that no human is alone. And then actionable steps.

When you have this opportunity to dream about what you want concerning your preferences, you can take the time to ask yourself which groups of people, gender, age, philosophy, you most enjoy. And, *why* they'd be interested in your topic. Write it down.

Everyone Is Not Your People

If you say your program, or the topic you want to teach is for everyone, you're missing the mark before you even begin to think about designing your program and marketing it. What you offer is NOT for everyone.

Your offerings will meet the needs of the world around you, but it's a big world, so break it down. With whom do feel your best? For your event to be successful, you don't *need* everyone to attend.

In the present chapter of my life, both personally and professionally, I really love a Women's Circle. After years of facilitating in all kinds of contexts, with all types of populations, including co-ed groups and one-on-one sessions, I've arrived to this realization by asking myself over and over who it is that I really *want* to spend time with and for whom I want to develop a workshop or retreat. Even after years of experience, it

---

[4] Carolyn Myss, Anatomy of the Spirit (New York, Harmony Books)

took some time for the answer to become crystal clear (because I enjoy a variety of people and leadership contexts).

But at the end of the day(s), when that little question seed has had enough time to expand under the ground state of my being, the answer continues to comes up: Women—mostly middle-aged—who love to learn and grow, explore facets of being, support one another, laugh, and <u>practice</u> what they've discovered is soulful life nourishment. That's what floats my professional boat.

What does *your* ideal population look like and *feel* like to you?

Get Specific, Don't Be Desperate

In your daydreams, you can and should get even more specific. In 2010 when I first began planning workshops and retreats for my (new) ideal population, women between 25 and 40, I felt desperate to fill my events and would invite every woman I knew. After years of filling Girls Rock! workshops to capacity, I had forgotten that *more* is not always better, and that business can and should take a little time to expand.

And naively, I thought:

Doesn't every woman want to relax and learn new self-care strategies for happiness and balance, and hang out with other dynamic women for a few hours to get away from stress, and play around with new strategies for well being?

Nope.

Every woman in my target population does *not*.

In other words, my desperation, naivety, and—hate to admit it—sloppy planning, were excellent learning experiences for me, helping me focus my approach and the growth of my leadership.

In one of my first wellness workshops for women, I included hula hooping as "a joyful movement feature" in the second hour of a half day retreat. But I hadn't advertised said hula hooping feature in the marketing material (yah, uh oh).

This did not go over so well for at least one participant (and by the way, this participant was a friend whose motivation to attend was completely tied to wanting to support my new mind-body health workshop effort— she was someone I knew well, who loved me and wanted my event to be a success).

But believe me when I say that no facilitator, new or seasoned, wants an expression of *You've got to be F!^#*^/! kidding me,* among her participants—friends or not. It can be a bit of a shake-up to one's confidence.

Roger that. Hula hooping lesson learned.

It's not that hula hooping is a bad idea. In fact, from a health and wellness standpoint, it's great for joint mobility, core strength building, and for releasing lymph stagnation to name a few benefits.

I was on the right track, baby. But, hula hooping, benefits or not, is not for everyone in a group setting. Surprise, or something unexpected in an unfamiliar environment, can cause a participant to feel vulnerable and trapped, even baited, among a group of strangers.

If you don't want a participant to say that she was the victim of a workshop-hula-hooping-attack, consider rethinking your approach. Don't spring anything unexpected on people even if you know and believe those features would "be great!"

There are people in your community who will want to engage in all the elements you dream up for a gathering, who need them and are looking for a holistic day of learning and experiences, but "every one I know" is not them.

When you sit down with your Idea Seeds Journal to play with ideas (by jotting down words and questions that come to you) it's helpful to picture the individuals who might represent your group of participants.

In my early Women's Circles, I didn't need to know each of my attendees ahead of time, but in the daydreaming stage of planning I could have crystalized a vision of who my participants were—what their needs and interests were, more than just "health and wellness." That way, the clarity of the event could have *attracted* my ideal customers—even if only five people registered out of my goal of 10.

Daydreaming is a sacred process in preparation, which feeds into practical stuff like expectations and accurate marketing strategies. When you dream and plan and advertise with a goal of clarity, if your participants aren't game when they arrive, it is not your problem: You've lived up to your responsibility of dreaming up something fabulous and can say with confidence:

Take it or leave it, sis.

How I Dream, Vision, and Plan It, Based on Theme

Here's an example of a journal musing on the topic of visioning the ideal participant within my target population. In a preparation session a few years ago, I knew I wanted to facilitate on the theme Animal Allies (a theme I've been mentored in), which is NOT for everyone's taste, but which I was excited to prepare and bring, and was excited for those who *would* attend.

Notice how the potential participants became clear to me from my theme:

- *Whatv: Symbolism theme for life's challenges. Soul Collage®*
  *Manifesting Personal Dreams. Using archetypal images as a
  resource. Fun to prepare. It's about knowing you're not alone on
  this "Earth walk"—life is hard but designed with helpers at every*

turn, meeting Spirit part way. Intersection of intentionality with Higher Power.

- <u>Who</u>: *This Circle will be for middle-aged women, 40's through 60's. Mature, open, like to share but not needy for attention in the Circle. Maybe women who know each other? It could be invitation only.*

  Picturing: Linda, R.T, Beth, Marnie, Jackie, Barbara, Erin, Jennifer, Frannie, Anne, Tatsiana, Erin, Cindi, Donna, and Donna, Debra, Lauren, Denise, and Deniese, Lynn (and women like them). They'd be excited to think about this theme, and gather their prep. images. Could open the Circle to friends of participants—repeat customers are trustworthy recruiters. Plus, meaningful for them to experience the gathering with a loved one.

- <u>How</u>: *SoulCollage®. Set up collage images on tables around the room. Participants can bring images too—but I'll have plenty on hand.*

- <u>Where</u>: *This would be SO GOOD at a nature center. Include a professionally guided hike in the tuition fee.*

Here, the theme musings got the ball rolling. I matched people with the specific theme and how they'd exist in the gathering space—how they'd benefit and contribute. These are important considerations.

Who are the people in your life, or extended community, you know will be excited about an event you put together?

Idea Seeds Journal: Muse with it.

Choosing and Marketing Theme Carefully

Sometimes your facilitation vision is connected to a particular group in your city. An example from my leadership facilitation: Underserved service professionals who need recovery tools from burn-out. Social Workers, Oncology Nurses, and Teachers come to mind. In this case, the vision would need to be very open to include a variety of people within the target population. Choice of theme and marketing would be careful, neutral, and generally appealing. Maybe the topic would be called: *Self-Care Strategies for The Over-Worked, Short on Time Service Professional.*

Those who attend would be looking for pragmatic self-care strategies.

If you were to market this theme, in your journal planning, your daydreams would include an open invitation to the public for anyone to see and to pass along. You might email some professionals directly and ask them to forward your invitation to people they know. But the language you use in advertising (and in person when leading this kind of workshop) would not include anything even vaguely "weird" or mystical in nature, or spiritual or religious. It's not the time nor population for it (no matter how sacred and spirit-guided a service you feel it could provide).

When I lead general public health and wellness events, I include my contact info on the hand-outs, and sometimes in my conclusion I'll add that I also lead more *intuition focused* curriculum through women's workshops and retreats, and invite participants to share their contact information to be included in my email invitations for this type of event. Frequently, I gain at least one new retreat attendee from these more general facilitation opportunities. Usually a few.

But I'm NEVER offended if no one says, "Me! Me! Me! Sign me up." I decided long ago that I have time only to think about marketing to people who'll be happy to receive an email from me about an event. I've released desperation. It was constricting.

Ironically, this release has brought success. My faith that people who want and need my programming will show up has enabled me to focus my program design and marketing. Most of my self-advertised events fill. And most participants are returning attendees now.

When I sit down to plan a gathering, on any theme, if I can't picture who it's designed for, the planning can't move forward properly. The seeds don't fully root. But if I push it anyway and an event does come together, I might end up with a *what the F^*!* expression in the second hour of the thing.

Once you picture the participant population to match your theme (or you imagine your theme to match your ideal population), and you're willing to NOT be desperate to attract everyone and anyone, the *how* and *where* will blossom from those sustainable roots.

Chapter 5

Confidence

Sometimes when I find myself feeling nervous or insecure about taking a creative risk in life, I will have this thought: "The women who came before me eliminated so many obstacles from my path...what a disgrace to their legacy it would be, if now I allow ME to become the only roadblock in my life."

~Shonda Rhimes

I Gotta Be Me and You Gotta Be You Ingredients

Now that you know who your ideal attendees would be, who will *you* be with them?

The answer to this begins with relaxing into the supportive tools you've gathered from your education. If you've been trained in some way as a facilitator, relax on the foundation of that. Trust that. And trust the qualifying organization. You are not an imposter. You did not fool your instructors or mentors into believing you could be trusted to facilitate their techniques and tools—you really can, and you have the experience to prove it (to yourself and anyone else who needs to know). You, like everyone else utilizing relevant resources can trust the process—the guidelines—given to you in your training.

There's an exciting intersection between you and subject matter of your leadership role. It's flavored with your passion for the topic/tradition/process you've studied. That intersection is where the h*art* and magic happen when implementing what you've learned. Only you can add an extra dash of flavor to the recipe in the sharing of it. Even if you are brand new to leadership, no one can offer exactly what you can, because no one has gathered the very same life experiences—wisdom ingredients—you have. No one has your perspective of the trivial and the profound: Everything you have done in your life, failed at, succeeded at, dreamed of. All of that counts toward the leader you will be in the room (or in the virtual space) with your attendees.

"Just be yourself" stands the test of time. This can't be overused or stated. It holds up. And you just gotta be you, every time, no matter the context. The extra dash you add as you lead, is you.

(As natural as it might be, refrain from swearing like a pirate in your facilitation setting.)

Who am I? is no longer a new question by this point in your (reading this book) life; if you feel some fear about facilitating your first gatherings, know that many before you have walked the very same path. That of leadership. We have all asked some of the very same deeply intimate questions about the *who am I* of leadership, and about the courage to do it. And we all keep asking, and doing, and figuring it out.

Just as you are now. Or still.

It can bring great comfort to know that fear and finding courage did not begin with you, that you are not alone in this; leadership has always begun, and will always begin with being prepared and showing up.

Strong leadership only requires practice.

Be Prepared, Show Up, Practice

You can do all those things: Be prepared, show up, and practice leadership at least twice, in order to notice how much better you'll feel the second time you facilitate. If you're a seasoned leader, it serves you to see how far you've travelled in your leadership journey, and to remember with humility how important is "beginners mind," still. For me today, taking stock and tracing improvements, and re-visiting humility, have been important upgrading tools as I strive toward new goals as a leader in mind-body health.

Who will I be as a facilitator? is a good question here. It serves you because it helps you to see yourself the way your attendees would. The way they do presently.

This is not a question to make you self-conscious, but to help you build your confidence so that you carry your realized strengths into the room when you enter—so that you own your strengths and enhance them, time and time again. How do you want your attendees to see you?

Years ago on one of my visits to spend time with my beloved mentors, Rosalyn and Ken, we women went shopping. It was spring and so, among all the bargains in the department store, we noticed the hat section generously stocked.

"Here, Lis, try this on."

I would never dream of turning down a directive from this woman who is a Goddess in my eyes, over 20 years my senior, and whose style is renown. But hats weren't my usual thing. In the mirror—in public—I felt embarrassed to look at myself and pose. With my shoulders hunched, I waited for Rosalyn to agree it looked stupid so I could take it off and move on.

"I look ridiculous."

Her response in the mirror was the raised eyebrow.

"What? This doesn't look ridiculous on me?"

And then: "Honey, wear it. Wear *it*. You're letting it wear you. *Own it* and see what happens. If you're gonna wear it, you gotta own it."

For Rosalyn's sake, and to make the hat horror end, I stood up straight to the mirror. Fixed my gaze. Hand on hip. I tried to own it. Quickly. My stance said, *I am a grown woman.*

She was right. I could own it. But I had to feel myself first. My own confidence. *Own* my own confidence. So that no matter what I put on, I'm the foundation beneath it.

As a leader, no matter what you offer, or say to your attendees, or blunder a little in the course of the gathering, it's all built on the solid foundation of your belief in at least some of your ability to pull it off. You don't even have to be fully confident; somewhat confident is enough. This confidence, even if it's just in the knowledge that you've been qualified to facilitate and have the skills and heart to carry the teachings forward, is what makes others feel comfortable in your company, and confident in you. Your confidence is what makes your attendees confident in *themselves* and confident to walk the path of the teachings you are offering. And to have the capacity to absorb them.

Personally, I don't have time to wait for confidence to find me. So on a day I'm not feeling it—maybe I'm venturing into unknown territory as facilitator or speaker, or some personal life thing is buzzing in the foreground of my thoughts, I remember three things to boost my confidence so that I'm doing something constructive to move closer to my *excellence in facilitation* goal. This is what I suggest:

1) Feel into who you've been, how you behaved, and where. What counts is what you said and even what you wore when you were successful with a goal—when you have *felt* confident.

   Each of us have plenty of personal examples in the memory bank. How you *have felt* counts because if you did anything with confidence before now, you can do something else with confidence, even if it's a different thing, today and tomorrow.

2) Remember to "own it." Just try to strike the symbolic confidence pose. I'm not talking about putting your hand on your hip, I'm

talking about standing up straight and looking people in the eyes, and smiling. Meeting your own experienced, grown-up-adult-woman reflection. Until it *feels* and *looks* true.

3) Remember to see yourself through the assuring eyes of someone whose qualities you admire, respect, and emulate. And whose no-nonsense, raised-eyebrow-voice sounds clear and confident in your own head. Your own capable internal voice can find the tone to ring in from there.

When you have that down—just your own internal work—you begin planting the seeds of cultivating and holding a sacred space.

All of this is the very h*eart*, sustenance, empowerment, and momentum, of leadership.

Chapter 6

Whom Do I Emulate?

*The women whom I love and admire for their strength and grace
did not get that way because shit worked out. They got that way
because shit went wrong, and they handled it. They handled
it in a thousand different ways on a thousand different days,
but they handled it. Those women are my superheroes.*

~Elizabeth Gilbert

Research Play Time Should Come With Snacks

N ow that it's clear that you can do this—that your current level of knowledge and willingness to show-up organized and with integrity is enough to get your leadership role started, you can play around with how you might strike your poses. It's crucial that you try to see yourself and your authority through the eyes of those who will be affected by your leadership demeanor.

If you're an experienced leader with a desire to take your events to the next level, you might play around with how you can add to the energy of your posture, authority, and relatability.

This is the fun part: Exploring the how and the why your favored presenters are effective. All you need is the internet, a pen and paper, and a comfortable seat. And snacks. This is research play time, dear reader friend.

Research play-time which looks at how admired people do it, will help you see *yourself* more clearly, not because you should compare your skills to theirs (pa-lease, no one but Gloria Steinem can be Gloria Steinem) but because you are still learning who and how you want to be as a leader. Or, you are refining your skills. Adding and upgrading.

Analyzing what you admire in others can shape your goals for yourself. This is always evolving.

But you must first be willing to acknowledge that you are evolving and growing your skills, and maintain some big faith that while you will never "do it" exactly as someone else, what and how you offer of yourself will be exactly how and what your attendees need. If they need Gloria Steinem exactly, they should go to her, exactly.

And no one can be you exactly, either.

1) Pick three people you find inspiring, or effective, or compelling. Choose among people you're already familiar with, whose work you've appreciated for some time—men and women. Or non-binary people. Watch and listen to a talk or presentation they each give, twice.

    (In video, I love TED Talks, You Tube, Oprah interviews, and David Letterman interviews. In podcasts, I love Krista Tippet interviews, Guy Raz interviews, and Ira Glass interviews. I love Richard Rohr's wisdom in every form. And Oprah, again, of course.)

First, just be present for the presentation. Enjoy it—let yourself be absorbed. At the end, articulate why you enjoyed it (yes, write it down. Good old Idea Seeds Journal, amiga. Or, speak it into a recording device). Off the top of your head, from that presentation, what are the lingering impressions that have you feeling inspired now that it's over?

2) Watch/listen again prepared to pause the presentation to make notes from the following questions:

    • What is she/he doing that I like?

- Is this visual presenter standing or sitting still, or moving around on the stage? Hand gesturing? Am I drawn to visuals like graphs and charts? Am I drawn to what the presenter is wearing?

- Is it basic story telling that I like? Or how the story is being told—the meaning behind the words?

- Is it articulate language that I'm drawn to, or is the story most important no matter the words chosen?

- OR, is it a combination of both?

- What else am I drawn to here?

- What little ticks or mannerisms stand out?

- What bothers me a little or a lot?

3) Finally, how would you describe this presenter to others? Imagine that you are telling a friend about why you like this person's presence on stage, and include what you would do differently—be descriptive and concise.

Using the guideline questions of (2) above, here's an example of my musings when I recently viewed an inspiring leader in medicine, Dr. Mark Hyman, on his professional Face Book page. I recommend subscribing to his page for up to date research in Functional Medicine and his interviews with leading experts:

1) **Why I enjoyed it**: *Easy-going, relatable leader. His voice and demeanor are pleasant. He's a renown medical practitioner— Cleveland Clinic, New York Times best selling author etc—AND he explains Functional Medicine with sincerity and humility. I appreciate his own personal story of illness and his path to health. Seems to live what he prescribes.*

2) **I like that**: *On his FB page broadcast he provides a platform for other experts. And then allows himself to be a student of their expertise.*

- *I like that on video he looks solid and comfortable. Sits up straight.*

- *That he's ready to chuckle with guest.*

- *Gestures are real: Hand on heart when discussing heart-centered issue. Smiles.*

- *Uses everyday language for the average non-medical viewer. Pleasant voice.*

3) **No thing I would do differently.**

- *Describing Dr. Hyman to a friend: Humble, present, affable, knowledgeable, capable, confident, authoritative, kind, good story teller. This is someone who is trained by rigorous standards and seems compelled to meld all of that with human emotional and spiritual health today.*

- *Role model of integrity.*

Love It, Live It, Give It

When I teach Eastern mind-body health practices to yoga teacher trainees, I invite them to absorb their experiences through the eyes of the teacher archetype—to stay awake to what is happening in themselves (physically, emotionally, mentally, spiritually), and awake to what's happening in the room as the teachings unfold. To notice what they like and dislike about the way the material is presented.

I encourage this way of learning because budding facilitators are training to take the temperature of the room and shift gears if a group is having trouble with a concept or direction; facilitation isn't just about communicating the material, it's about meeting participants where they are so that they can occupy a space *with* the material. Where its inherent light can be appreciated heart-fully (sometimes physically and spiritually), as well as understood (mentally).

I find that many students grasp the totality of the learning experience that way rather than myopically with just a goal of being able to facilitate a specific concept or curriculum.

As a perpetual student myself, this strategy truly works for me in the style of Ekhart Tolle, *Power of Now*: Be in the experience *and* the objective observer of the experience. I enjoy attending live events of all sorts and can't help but bring my conscious awareness to my participation as an attendee. I'm submerged in the experience while also aware of my participation in it. And I notice how and why live presenters effect my affect.

Allow yourself to be the witness of your own participation. You might find that the state of your emotions inform your ability to remember what you've learned, and to feel passion about passing it on.

That's right, *you've* got to love it, to live it, to give it.

Write down the nuances of your experience soon afterward, while it's still fresh.

Whatever your research involves, virtual, recorded, live, once you engage in this objective (and subjective) research, you should have a pretty articulated idea of what you appreciate in other presenters. None of us will be, nor should we try to be, anyone other than who we are, but analyzing the qualities we admire and dislike in other presenters is useful toward becoming the best version of ourselves, eventually.

Finally, in the continuing conversation about confidence and finding inspiration from others who smooth the path here, I recommend watching Lidia Yuknavitch's 2016 Ted Talk: The Beauty of Being a

Misfit. In some minor and major ways, you might see yourself in Lidia. Her courage (and former lack of it) can help you examine the ways of your own unnecessary self-imposed limitations. You will say out loud to her video presentation, "What were you thinking? Of course you were good enough. Look at the clues!" By the end, you'll inwardly cheer her triumph. Hopefully, you'll see yourself in triumph too. Let her story reassure you of your own worthiness, because we human beings are all the same, even if only a little.

Chapter 7

Poise, Professionalism, Kindness

"Rather than thinking in terms of good and bad, it is more helpful to think in terms of conscious and unconscious, aware, and unaware."

~Joan Borysenko,

Straight Up, Partner

While we humans are intuitive beings, many of us sensitive of spirit—who even have conversations *with* Spirit—are also pragmatic, practical, professional people. Maintaining a professional leadership standard that will provide credibility among colleagues, strangers, and attendees, should always be intentional.

So here comes some pragmatic, practical, professional straight talk—some Must Do's as a leader in every context ever, no matter who you've emulated so that you can identify the general standards most respected leaders abide in the context of service. Because, whether you facilitate in the woods next to a stream, in a yoga studio or retreat center, in a civic center auditorium or other stage, or from a doctor's office, professional standards apply to you in your role as a leader/facilitator while you're "on."

Poise and Professionalism

It's likely that none of the leaders you chose to analyze for effectiveness, demonstrated their secret worry about not doing justice to the topic or task at hand. If you are worried about your effectiveness, do not say you are worried. If you're not feeling well but have shown up anyway, do not say you're not feeling well. If someone in your family is ill, or you're feeling devastated over world affairs, or if you are nervous, do not say anything about any of that—even if you believe that everyone can tell.

Mum's the word, my girlfriend.

You, like everyone on this planet, are human with human vulnerabilities. But if you have chosen to show up to facilitate despite your challenged emotional and physical feeling-states, you must leave your challenges outside of your leadership space. As a facilitator, your number one priority is professionalism and your attendees' benefit. Those in your presence are automatically vulnerable to what you share because they have come with an open heart—you owe it to your audience to offer only the smartest and wisest of your voice, feeling state, and experience.

Recently, I attended an event in a house of worship; I had looked forward to it for weeks. There were two dozen people in attendance—we had all reserved our participation in advance. I could tell from the buzz in the room before the speaker picked up the microphone that everyone was excited about this presenter who had travelled from Europe to teach.

But in his opening remarks, the very first thing he said was, "I am terribly jet-lagged, I hope you will excuse me if I seem tired."

"Nooooooooooooooooooooooooooo," was all I could think in my head, "Don't say thaaaaaaaat."

NOOOOOOOOOOOOOOOOO.

I had looked forward to this presentation for weeks, why oh why would he ruin the buzz in the room, all set up for him to step so fluidly into? Why would he ruin his own chances at effectiveness?

Why ruin *my* buzz?

Essentially, everything he said after this introduction, for the duration of the 60 minute program, rested directly upon the shaky foundation HE laid at our feet. From his admitted exhaustion, could we even trust his presentation now?

But he did provide the perfect book-end for his introduction; in his conclusion he said this from the podium: "I hope this presentation wasn't too boring."

As an attendee, here's my feeling about this leadership behavior: Don't make me worry about your well-being. And for Goodness Sake, don't make me want to take care of your needs. I am in your care—whether you are my taxi driver, health-professional, contractor, teacher, presenter, performer, facilitator—and I expect you to bring your best energy.

I prefer you *try* to be confident, rather than admit that you are struggling.

When I'm in the audience, I do not expect perfection, and I don't expect leaders to be anything but human, but I do expect professionalism, and I expect to feel that I'm in good hands. Whether I'm watching a recorded Dalai Lama dharma talk from home (so fulfilling and nourishing), am in the audience at a Melissa Etheridge concert (so inspiring and fun), or in a classroom, or sitting one-on-one with a therapist, I am receiving and digesting the energy that takes the stage—cultivates the space.

If just before surgery, your surgeon admits to you that she is tired, you should get right up off that table. Because it's very reasonable to not trust anything she does surgically after that admission.

By the same token, when a participant is in your care (whether it's a one-on-one, or in an audience among dozens or hundreds or thousands) she does not want to be drawn into your own personal issues either. Not even something as minor as being tired.

Luckily, facilitating, performing and presenting are not surgery. There will be times you'll be facilitating with very little reserve in your tank, but unlike in a pre-surgery situation, you're under no obligation to divulge that, nor do you want participants to lose faith in you. Nor do you want them to be energetically drawn-in to your poor feeling state. Nor do you want to set up a sustaining tiredness energy for yourself in the space by articulating it—nor make others soak up your exhaustion!

I've given presentations and led workshops under mental and physical duress. For varying reasons, cancelling would have been worse than showing up.

Choosing to go on with the show means putting your best face and best energy forward for those in your energy field.

As my mentor Rosalyn might say, "Tuck it in."

Yes, do that, you have important things for your attendees and for yourself, to focus on. As a leader, your time with participants should be emotionally *clean*. It's not their job to reassure you that you're acceptable and effective.

Do I sound strict on this?

Well shucks, you flatter me.

Mistakes and Kindness and Humor

As you're facilitating, if you are organized and prepared, and if you want your events to be fulfilling experiences for you and all, it's very likely that most of the time things *will* go your way.

And, sometimes they will *not*.

That is life. Shit happens. And then it should become *shit happened*—as in past tense—because your intention should be to learn from whatever happened and move forward. Your only response to shit happens should be kindness and humor—for yourself and others.

Here are some real-life *shit happens* events within my events, where I was the main leader responsible for all of it, and here's how things got resolved by moving on swiftly on all levels of the physical, the mental, and then the symbolic levels of being a humanoid.

Story #1 It Was About a Gallon

Something spilled. A great deal of it. I had put out a jug of water with a spigot for attendees. It was the first time I had put out a jug of water that size (5 gallons) because about 50 people were attending. At other events I had watched coordinators slash the top of the jug to release air pressure allowing water to flow from the spigot below with more force.

Because I am pretty organized (and a little compulsive—I make a list of things to bring and check them before I'm out the door), I remembered to bring a pocket knife. And in the tradition of other big-water-jug-coordinators, I slashed.

But I should'a poked. Or stabbed lightly.

A lot of water flowed from the TOP of the jug. But I didn't notice because I had walked away to take care of other details in the 30 minutes before the introductory remarks. In that time, A LOT of water, nearly a gallon, had time to ruin all the paper plates, napkins, fliers and brochures on both sides of the jug, on the table.

It was a group of attendees streaming in who noticed and alerted me. I was embarrassed in front of a room full of attendees, but the good news was that there was a room full of attendees who moved into action wielding paper towels from the bathroom, and a mop from the storage closet, and a trash can for lost-cause paper goods and brochures.

What could I do? I went with it. Because I could not turn back time. So, in my introductory remarks from the microphone I thanked everyone for the help and made a joke about how the success of a gathering really and truly is in the "wet hands" of everyone who shows up. And then I made a pitch for group cohesion among women—how something even trivial like this happens just to prove that women show up to support one another even when they didn't expect their contribution would matter to anyone.

Find the gold in the dark, no matter what. Good advice for leadership. And for life.

When you're open to being playful with "mistakes" they look a lot less like mistakes and just more like relatable life things. With practice, this will come more easily.

I did not plan to be so witty and thoughtful about it. But I did plan to refrain from whining and over apologizing for it. Because my mind-set in my *off hours* with my Idea Seeds Journaling had been to "go with the flow" no matter what, witty and thoughtful found me in the middle of my event. And help from attendees did too.

The Lesson: Go with the flow of whatever happens. It'll probably be useful to do so.

Story #2 Change Direction, Improvise

Have you ever lost an entire power-point presentation between leaving home and arriving to *your* venue? Even though you boast an organization streak? I have. And my entire team too. But I was the only grown-up on the team, and the one responsible—the responsible face of the program.

When I founded and coordinated Girls Rock! Workshops for Girls and Moms, I trained teen mentors to help facilitate the programming which included a media literacy hour where we showed popular advertising images and opened a Q & A with participants about how inherent messages shape self-esteem.

But the lead teen in charge of the power-point, who brought the computer, could not find the power-point anywhere on her computer.

And my boastful pre-event organization list managed to be sloppy this time—I got out the door without my digital copy as a back up.

14 moms and 14 daughters sat patiently awaiting the opening program as we searched our supplies high and low. They waited patiently for 15 minutes while we searched (and while I counted every passing second of this delay). We searched. And searched.

Finally, I had to call it and change direction. The initial delay could not be helped (and I am originally Canadian—always prompt—lateness that can not be "helped" is a generous concept to begin with).

The show must always go on.

I turned to my last resort back up to the back up, which I had managed to bring: a multi-page, colored-paper copy of the Power Point.

There!

One by one, the teen team held up each pale single 8x10 paper version of the big bright screen digital images they'd constructed, and taught from them.

Was it as impressive and clear as a big screen version of the images narrated by seven teen presenters effortlessly stepping in to take turns with the script? No it was not. Was every audience member able to see those paper 8x10 versions as clearly as they would have a big screen version. No they could not. Did that matter?

No it did not.

Why? Because after instructing my team to be light-hearted about it, all of it, and just move on quickly, they rose to it.

Only we, The Team, knew how impressive it *could have* been. The audience, presented with the program for the first time, were happy to have it. They moved their seats to see better. The teachings were compelling enough no matter their presentation. Moms and daughters learning together was special, and it was spectacular when brought to them by teen girls passionate about the subject matter.

Power Point, Power-shmoint. Don't let 'em see you sweat.

When you're open to improvising, your "mistakes" will feel a lot less like problems and just more like a do-able new direction. With practice, this will come more easily.

The influence of your teachings, if they are trust-worthy, and if you believe in them, will have an impact that is beyond your doing anyway. Show up to be a channel for the work you are presenting—take less blame for what goes wrong that can't be helped, and less credit for the successes that "go right" (which will help you stay off the pedestal, and, will prevent you from falling from one if people put you there).

Within the group you serve, you are the initial cultivator of the sacred; life is the bigger force that calls you to go with it.

Lesson: No one else knows how good your program "could have been."

Chapter 8

Healthy Boundaries and Non-Attachment

*Between stimulus and response there is a space. In
that space is our power to choose our response. In our
response lies our growth and our freedom.*

~Viktor Frankl

Being Responsible Includes Being NOT Responsible

No matter the theme or teachings, it is not your responsibility, I repeat, not your responsibility, to rescue your attendees from their own problems.

You are the bringer of information, the setter upper and holder of the sacred space, the conductor of the harmony. But you can not control the harmony. You can't control how out-of-tune someone is when they join your gathering.

It's important to know this now, in the early planning stages of your gathering, so that this truth can be integrated into your core understanding of healthy leadership and the personal and professional boundaries built within. Eventually, when you step into your facilitation space, this knowing will *be* you. Even if you're leading a group up a mountain in a raggedy line.

As facilitating leaders, of course we want everyone to have a positive experience, but others' experiences are not within our regulation. You can *influence* but you can not control how, or if, or why, someone will integrate or even accept what you bring. Each of us maintain responsibility to our own experiences. You have yours, and your attendees have theirs.

Earth School Paradoxes and Stuff

As human beings we are here, living in and through these physical bodies and backgrounds which are also personality shapers—perspective shapers. Based on the lens of experience, life is colored a certain way: the environment, and people, and relationships, and expectations about success and failure, love and hate, worth and worthlessness. One hundred people can have one hundred varying perspectives of the very same conversation, event, relationship.

While the dramas and details of our human lives are fleeting, growth from those up-and down challenges are enduring.

From Gary Zukav's, wonderful *The Seat of the Soul*, we see that it's all about an individualized personal life curriculum:

"Ask what you are feeling and what is at the root of it. Go for the root of it in that instant and, as you work to pull the root, simultaneously look at the positive side and remind yourself of the greater truth that there is something spiritually profound at work, that your life is no accident, that you are under contract."[5]

The paradox of good life things and "bad" are essential in the grand scheme of things for all of us—including people who appear to be having a hard time. What if being in the muck for a spell brings some unconscious issue to light? What if the dark mucky discomfort is actually the prerequisite for the joy class in someone's Earth School curriculum?

---

[5] Gary Zukav, Seat of the Soul (New York, Simon & Schuster) pg. 233

From a larger perspective here, as a facilitator, you are not going to understand the deep *why* someone in your workshop is "struggling" the way they are. Even if you've been trained by evolved healers, the profound *why* is between an individual and Higher Power. Most of the time, we have a limited understanding of the spiritual meaning and purpose of our own trivial and serious struggles; it's not possible to fully understand the mysteries of others'.

It is possible though, that a "miserable looking" or "ill" or "defeated" or "needy" participant is experiencing something essential for the growth of her soul. As leaders and therapeutic arts facilitators, we don't even know *what we don't know* about someone else's life journey.

Your job is to hold a sacred space—a potential—for people to learn and grow and heal. You can't do their work for them. Again, this is the heart of your leadership.

Unless someone at your event confides that she is living in a dangerous environment, stay lovingly out of her business—even if she complains about it. It is her responsibility to pull up the root of truth for herself.

Your Rescue Glasses

In a general facilitation context, when you see a person who "needs" aromatherapy, or body work, or access to vegetables, or quality sleep, or a healthier marriage, or or or or or, you are seeing that person through the lens of your own needs. You are not the messianic bringer of solutions for healing for an individual, or for every body in the room. Time to change your prescription, gf.

Donna, my dear friend, a Registered Dietician who's specialized for 25 years in eating disorders intervention, puts it this way: "Rescuing interferes in someone else's destiny. And it interferes in yours."

The role of the leader is to be a source of compassion and Light, not a fixer, even though you care so much. If over and over when you're facilitating, you have a desire to fix or rescue someone from their pain, be aware that your desire is about a need that you have, not a deficiency that they have.

AND/BUT, it is your job to have confidence that everyone can rise to the occasion of the sacred growth and transformation space that you've cultivated, which continues to deepen with attendee participation. As the sacred space cultivator and holder—the responsible source of compassion and Light at said event—your attendees have an opportunity to meet *you* in that place.

I read that in the Grand Poobah Universal Facilitator Handbook for Dummies.

(Jk, I haven't read it yet, I just know it has to be in there.)

Projection Protection

Knowing deeply that professional fixing is not in your job description—and behaving accordingly—will also help to protect you from the occasional projections that come from attendees who *think* you should be *their* life preserver jacket because you "carry so much Light and knowledge", and because you have "the magic pill" for their pain.

And because you are the most beautiful and funny and smart and slightly sarcastic badass facilitator they've ever met.

Or until next month, when the next compassionate and shiny leader catches their eye.

I can assure you that there are not enough life preserving floatation devices in the universe to fix or save a desperately grasping friend or family member, client or workshop-er, or audience member. Or, ahem, reader. Rather, saving efforts might placate a grasping spirit temporarily, but until she makes the decision to save herself, utilize resources to work on her pain and needs, she will resume sinking into her own problems and influences shortly thereafter. Your lifesaving efforts would be poured down a bottomless ravine.

Again, as leaders, it's our responsibility to make room for attendees' potential, and then within that space to offer therapeutic tools for self-care and transformation. It's not within the parameters of that responsibility to make them work for others.

I find it helpful to be plugged into community resources, to know about the best professional helping agencies and therapists and spiritual leaders and medical professionals in town, and to refer when it seems appropriate. That's what I can do to help when there's an obvious need— hand it over.

It might sound like this:

Participant #1 (who brings up her failing marriage for the third time in a group exercise):

"I just don't want that asshole to affect my life anymore!"

Facilitator: "That's a powerful statement. I'm noticing that your marriage has been a reoccurring theme for you today. If you're interested, and feel that some on-going support would be helpful, please let me know later—I could email you some excellent resources that I know of in our community.

Participant #2: "Please share that resource with me too if you don't mind."

Participant #1: "No thanks."

And then, be okay with the referral snub.

Empowerment and Victimhood

When something really really good happens, I can say, 'I did that!'
And when something really really bad happens, I can say, 'I did that!

~Esther Hicks

It bears repeating that you *own* your own experiences, and others own theirs.

As leaders, it's a pleasure and a calling to create the space for participants to discover their personal answers and *aha* moments. Remember how vital and transformational your revelations were for you when you became awake to them? Perhaps an inspiring leader opened a door for you, but, you made the choice to walk through it toward your own transformation. No one could have done that for you.

I feel empowered by my decisions to live healthfully, and fortunate to have been exposed to questions around "life quality." That exploration enabled me to adopt better habits and choices. Intentional choices created greater emotional bandwidth. While I can list inspiring mentors and leaders a page long, not one of them made it possible for me to adopt the habits I now live. I did that, it's my credit to own.

And, my poor choices are mine to own too; it's empowering to know and live this truth.

"Bad things" and "bad circumstances" did not randomly find me over and over. They weren't random. This knowing plucks me out of victimhood and places me solidly with the power of choice.

In my twenties and thirties, I frequently ended up in the proximity of angry people: people with road rage, hostile strangers at the grocery store, belligerent customer service representatives on the phone. When I had the courage to realize that all those diverse people in diverse contexts had one thing in common, me, I could begin to have a say in the energy around me by having a say about the energy in me, first. From me.

What was I feeling, thinking, saying, and expecting about life that made those circumstances pop up in my experience time and time again? How was I shortchanging myself by not being aware of my own energetic contribution to those "random" events?

With the help of a wonderful specialist, Gene, now my long time psychotherapist, I chose to work on my own rage. While the traumas of my life hadn't been my "fault" they certainly were my responsibility to heal if I wanted my life to reflect enduring health and joy. Especially for my young daughters to emulate. Over nearly 20 years, Gene's help has been impactful on every level of my human health being-ness.

But while he has always been a helper of my little and great transformations, he maintains that he deserves no credit—that it's been his job (I say *calling*) to support and reflect potential, but not to make it happen.

Gene never took responsibility when my choices led to misery—though I'm certain he preferred that I feel well. By the same token, Gene took no credit for my better choices. He was (and lovingly continues to be) the holder of my potential, not the one responsible for it either way.

Influence, not control. There it is again. This has been a great gift to me emotionally, and professionally. I emulate this in all my personal and leadership roles.

When your attendees are empowered to "own" their own negligence around life habits—thoughts, feelings, behaviors, and the energy they emit—they are no longer victims of anything in present time.

Ownership of personal agency and consequences, positive and not, is determined by each of us.

And, as Rabbi Kushner wrote in his bestseller, *When Bad Things Happen to Good People,* randomly terrible things sometimes do occur—it too is life. I'm not referring to that here. My point is about the empowerment of ownership of one's pervasive outlook and the consistent life decisions and experiences that emerge from that view. It's as empowering for people to own their "mistakes" as their successes.

Cultivating and holding a space is sacred work; set it up, keep an eye on it, and get out of the way. If you do that, you'll be a good facilitator. A very good leader.

The Solution to Pollution Is Dilution, and a School of Fish

Not being deeply attached to participants' experiences and growth allows a harmonious bigger focus to emerge in the group space. This can have a miraculous effect where the energy of the "straggling, struggling" participant is concerned (the one who can have a dragging effect on others in the space and can trigger you to over empathize), because that poor energy becomes diluted.

Another way to look at this: The disharmonious one naturally aligns with the bigger group energy present, often without any awareness that this is happening. Eventually, someone taking up a lot of energetic space in a group (talking a lot, moving too slowly, or hyper-active, or brooding etc.) becomes much more pleasant to be with. Falls in line.

Imagine a school of fish traveling with ease in one direction. The forces of nature that rotate planets and maintain an organized balance in the cosmos is the very same intelligent force that compels a school of fish underwater to travel with ease in one direction toward safety and food. This is the same intelligence alive in you, that helps you know when to change direction in your life. It is much bigger than any one planet, or fish, or human you.

When a school moves past one lost fishy, the entire school, dozens of fishes strong, doesn't stop to examine the straggler. Rather, the lost one is compelled toward its greater good, to move in stride with the school—the force of the group energy—and also, it's own highest good. Flow.

A straggler doesn't ask permission to no longer be lost and struggling. A natural instinct kicks in and the lost one is just swept up in the current of the entire school—she is pulled toward, within, and along. No longer stands out. Is no longer in desperate need. The volition of the group has elevated her status from lost, needy, poor, and "off", to moving in the right direction, toward sustenance and security.

The solution to pollution is dilution, and, the biggest aura wins. Always.

We have Rev. Rosalyn Bruyere again, a modern day oracle, to thank for demonstrating and capturing these pithy truths.

As a facilitator, if you prepare yourself (all the good stuff of Part I of this book: seeded goals, training and resources, self-care, an understanding of healthy boundaries, a meditation practice, and a relationship with Spirit), and if you prepare the energy of cultivating a sacred space ahead of time, you won't have much "work to do" on the day of your event. The sacred space will help take care of the harmony itself. Will help bring everyone up to speed to meet their own potential.

All those potentials combined, elevate the group in a way you can't predict with your human abilities. And importantly, all that preparation will help you maintain the biggest aura in the room until the highest-good group-energy kicks in.

Again, leadership is sacred work.

Non Attachment and Sacred Facilitation

Next to the healthy-boundaries mind set of this entire chapter so far, is the non-attachment mind set.

Aparigraha, a Sanskrit word, is also a vital principle, the last Yama in Patanjali's Eight Limbs of Yoga. It often translates to *non-greed* and *non-attachment*. It's one of the central teachings in the Bhagavad Gita, a Hindu text full of metaphors for living a life of balance in which Krishna, a central character, shares one of the teachings that could perhaps be the most important lesson of all:

Let your concern be with action alone, and never with the fruits of action. Do not let the results of action be your motive, and do not be attached to inaction (BG 2.47).

Though non-attachment is an ancient principle, it's gained much traction in our modern day approach to human "Earth school" perspectives, healthful boundaries, and personal responsibility.

Non-attachment does not mean that you don't care what happens in your gathering, or how your participants feel and experience what you offer, it means that you have accepted that you can do your best, but once again, you can not control the outcome no matter how well-seeded your intentions, dreams, prayers, and plans. It means aim high, be okay if you miss. And be okay if others miss.

Be cool, yo.

The principles of aparigraha—non-attachment—can guide your facilitation this way: Pledge to maintain healthy boundaries, to show-up in the best possible ways because you have done your homework, but that you won't get wrapped up in how things turn out.

No matter how well you hold up your end of: Responsibility, intuition, and the professionalism-bargain you've made, letting go of outcome will interestingly, paradoxically, set up a best outcome energy for you, and with you in the flow of events. This happens because you make room for something much bigger than yourself to take up residence in you as the leader, and in the space where you have gathered people.

Whatever that something much bigger is, you are the real live human vehicle of it—warts and beauty, and all. I hope this doesn't feel overwhelming or scary, because if you feel called to leadership and are reading here, it's likely you are a facilitator of good of some sort, why not consider how you're offering your hands, voice, skills, and heart as a benevolent extension of Higher Power? Why not consider the truth that you are engaging in a sacred practice of facilitation? And that you can eventually step into it with ease—like all things that practice affords you?

Gene used to say to me, "Lisa, consider how you might be God's hands in the world right now, not later when you earn a better title, and not later when you think you'll be perfect at this or that..." His perspective and reassurance were invaluable. Still are.

So, I say this to YOU now:

You there with integrity, if you have something to share, Life wants to meet you where you are and work through you for the benefit of others, and for your own growth. It'll help you to gain more confidence through your training and use of resources. But either way, expect miracles at every phase of this leadership thing. Don't narrowly search for them; don't be disappointed if they don't reveal themselves immediately: practice non-attachment. But revel in them when they show up.

And most importantly, consider how you might be God's hands in the world right now, not later when you earn a title, and not later when you think you'll be perfect at something. Right now. Right now. Just begin where you are.

Healthy boundaries, empowerment, the solution to pollution is dilution, non-attachment, miracles: It's all Earth School, baby! It's all soul growth. For everyone. All the time.

Chapter 9

Self-Care, A Recipe for You and You and You

The first thing I do every single morning is pray. (Specifically, I pray to be relieved from the bondage of self.) Then I meditate. Then I dance. Then I write myself a letter from Love. (This is the most important part of my day, when I connect to Love herself, and ask her what she would have me know today.) Then I do the Work of Byron Katie, a worksheet on stressful beliefs.

~Elizabeth Gilbert

Ingredients and Dosing

My friend, Rhonda, agrees whole-heartedly with the prescription to, "Make a list of things that help keep you physically, emotionally, mentally, and spiritually healthy. When you're struggling, look at your list. Take your own medicine. Done."

Your self-care, long before you arrive to facilitate your event, will make you a better facilitator, speaker, friend, co-worker, leader. An odd myth that gets a lot of attention today is that self-care is a luxury. And selfish.

But how would the self that is you have enough verve to do anything without an identifiable, reliable, regularly practiced self-care routine?

When you were a kid, someone took care of those needs for you—(hopefully) provided security, food, hygiene, fresh air, play, socialization, and most importantly, love. The basics of your survival and growth were not a "luxury" when they were provided you, but according to Maslow's Hierarchy of Needs they were the foundational basis of your ability to appropriately and confidently function in the world around you. And I would add, within you.

The fulfillment of basic needs allows human beings to thrive and to live up to true potential—the full expression of one's soul from the vantage point of a human experience.

Nowhere in any modern health literature or perennial wisdom teachings does it say that there is a time in one's life journey when it's no longer necessary to continue to expect security, food, hygiene, fresh air, play, socialization, and most importantly, love.

As adults we're supposed to have learned to continue implementing those primary necessities for ourselves—for the continuation of our species. And to keep taking the sustenance that grew us, as well as provide it for the next generation, or anyone in our care.

You know you wouldn't purposely omit flour or sugar from a cake. If you omit one or two of your basic life ingredients, you're gonna know it—in the form of outcome—in the quality of your life experiences.

Am I right?

Just as the quality of your cake will suffer, or it'll fail to rise at all, so will the quality of your life.

The beauty of adulthood is that each of us gets to decide what and how much of each of those basic life self-care ingredients are right. Each of us needs a specific dosing of those ingredients. *What* and *how much*, and *when*, are vital self-care questions; they are *the* vital self-awareness questions. Once you figure that out, those ingredients making up your own life-recipe become part of your DNA.

For me for example, adequate sleep is vital. So is a quiet living environment. Laughter with my husband, and friends. Loving touch.

Time out in nature. Time with family. Fresh vegetables and fruits. Physical movement. Prayer and meditation. Creative outlets (lots). Learning (lots and lots). Teaching. Beauty in art and nature, and the human spirit. Adventure here and there.

All of these things are ingredients in my sustaining, nourishing, life-recipe. It took me some time to identify those ingredients and more—necessary in my hierarchy of needs—but now that I have, I notice when some are missing because I start to feel it. Wither a bit. Feel some blah blobbiness. When I'm under (life ingredient) nourished in some way, I don't enjoy my own company, I don't feel inspired about much, and I'm no fun to be around. In that case, my contribution to my own happiness, to my intimate relationships and to my facilitative leadership roles, is *meh*, or okay, instead of terrific. I can get by on so-so, but why should I?

Why should you?

Rising to your own occasion as a leader is not about the immediate moments preceding your goal, it's about the habits in the weeks (maybe months and years) before.

This is great news! You can take your time. Success when it happens will be a smooth transition.

So, take your own medicine. Done.

Lean on External Motivations When You Need 'Em

While it would be ideal to be internally motivated toward self-care at all times—in other words, to be perpetually motivated because of a strong inner drive to be as healthful as possible—sometimes you just gotta use whatever motivation's available in the moment, like, *love the one you're with* (thank you very much, Crosby, Stills & Nash).

External motivations can at times be an excellent force for good in your emotional well to keep things aimed at terrific, rather than in the *meh* category.

My roles as a mother, partner, teacher, facilitator, and leader, are my external motivations to take care of myself—to make sure I take all my life-recipe ingredients in adequate doses—in order to show up fully in those roles.

And to show up for myself.

Respect toward those external motivations keep me on track because they make me try when I don't think I have the energy to try. I stack up all the people affected by me in all those roles and I know with certainty they *would* in fact give a shit if I quit.

Accordingly, on the low internal motivation days, I *just do it*. It's my Nike Olympics of external motivation. And it always works: I do it until I feel better and until I want to do it to satisfy myself internally.

Higher Octane Sustenance

If you want to truly enhance the quality of your own life, do more than show up, feel on most days happy and grateful and excited to be alive, I can tell you that external motivation and "adequate" dosing of life ingredients is not enough.

There are things in your life that feed your soul and make your heart sing. What are they? They are your TRUEST power source.

For example, if you know that creativity and making things have always been your "happy place"—that art makes you lose track of time along with the 15,000 things you tend to worry about, but you are too "busy" or "don't have enough room" to even fiddle with something on your kitchen table, or in your notebook—you are short changing your own spirit. Causing your own depletion.

Hello, your happy place *is* vital nourishment for you, Human Being, you.

If you don't engage in your life sustaining needs and callings, you are depleting yourself in the same way you can be nutritionally depleted without vitamins from food. Even cutting yourself off from Source. God. Non-local Infinite Intelligence.

My sister and I always joke that we should needlepoint (or paint, or decoupage, or bead embroider) the following statement onto a pillow:

If I can't wake up in the morning excited about the new thing I'm making, what's the point of living?

Though my sister and I love our families and our roles in them, and our professional work, and nature in summer, and travel, and a great meal, and, and, and… All of those important things are fleeting.

But always present, and true, and reliable, is the joy we each feel when engaged in crafting. We are never more sustained and connected with our own souls—over prolonged period of hours and years—than when "in" the creation process.

For me, it's a place to co-create. It's a God place, even when what I'm working on is a silly experimental thing and the outcome is not great. The destination isn't always important. It's the process; the filling in between the cookie ends that can be deliciously fulfilling.

Let's look at it this way: Your car, like your body, houses a myriad of parts that together make it possible for you to get from A to B smoothly. Your engine, the most important part of all the parts, which "drives" the entire car system, relies on several things to keep it functioning. I'm not educated in car mechanics but I do know that one of the most important make-the-engine-work necessities is gasoline. Without gas, there's no getting from <u>start</u> to a <u>destination</u>. Without gas, turn on your engine: nada.

Or worse, you run out in the middle of the highway.

The engine of your self is your physical body and your emotional body and your mental body and your spirit. *What* you feed these systems is vital, just as your car will not accept gasoline substitutes such as juice, or olive oil, or vinegar. As useful a thing as vinegar is, it is not what your engine needs.

Your *self* can not be expected to run on poor substitutes either.

However, because of the nature of innate human survival, we do possess something that inanimate objects like cars do not: Will. Human *will* can sometimes outrun (out drive) a rundown system, pushing it to move when no logical reasoning can explain how it's possible a person can still be alive when existing on a life diet without enough rest, food, love, passion, with just vinegar in the tank.

However to that however is this: For MOST human beings, the deficit of loving, personal provisions will starve the multi-faceted engine of self, yearning for meaning, purpose, and reliable health.

As a leader, the quality of personal health not only affects the engine, it affects the viability of the tank feeding the engine. It affects everyone in the vicinity of fumes.

Make a List, Take Action

How?

I really like journal lists and recommend them. I make them pretty regularly, and I facilitate their use in all my teaching and facilitating contexts: women's retreats, cancer support groups, co-ed workshops, and yoga teacher training modules.

Lists bring clarity. And then they can be used as tools moving forward. This is a good time to make one. What can you identify as needs, specific to you, on each level of your being?

To get you started, I suggest the Sustenance Map:

Draw a circle on poster board, or in the middle of a page in your Journal. Put yourself in the circle—write your name as a place holder. Draw four long lines from your name in the center of your circle toward each corner of your page. At the end of each line respectively, write the headings: **Physical, Emotional, Mental, Spiritual**. Under each of those headings, list the five things you consider vital nourishment and maintenance. What are your non-negotiable needs in each category?

For many adults, what was provided in childhood were the vital basics; in adulthood, what is identified and chosen now, are vital fine-tuned basics that must be managed by said adult.

Further questions for your meditative lifestyle (enjoyable to muse over while walking your dog, or your baby, or your partner, or llama, or your quiet self) are:

What do I need? What sustains me? In what areas of my life do I want or need help? Where can I find help? How do I want to feel? How do I want others to feel around me? What does that look like for me right now? What can that look like for me? What makes my heart sing?

As a leader, I know others will learn from me because...

Explore this for yourself as well for the others you're externally motivated to influence. Fill your own tank with the quality ingredients you've identified as essential for you, and enough of them, so that not only do you not run (drive) the risk of running out of gas, but so that you are full enough—yes, so full of yourself—that you can give to others from your overflow.

Don't Slack Off

I talked to a friend at a party recently—we hadn't seen in each other in months—she offered that she'd been neglecting herself:

"Neglecting? How?" I asked.

"It's a little like the person who takes their meds to fight depression, feels better and then stops taking them," she said.

"What! Don't fuck with that! Take your meds! I love you and want you to be the healthiest version of yourself. I want you to want that," I said.

Self-care is selfish? Well, yah, what else would it be? If you are ever accused of being "selfish", the appropriate response is:

You are most welcome, loved ones.

Chapter 10

Rooted Joy and Wisdom = Success

*It's only when we truly know and understand that we
have a limited time on earth—and that we have no way of
knowing when our time is up—that we will begin to live
each day to the fullest, as if it was the only one we had.*

~Elizabeth Kubler Ross

Play in and With Your Work and Carry-On Together

When I sit down with pen and paper to "work" with ideas and
inspiration for an event that I'm getting ready to facilitate, it's a lot
more play than work, actually. My best workshops, trainings, and retreats
are the result of *playing around* with ideas. It is a focused process—tuned
in and absorbed in the theme or the question about it—but my approach
is joyful and light. A time to dream about possibilities and how those
potentials might look, and brainstorming with my Idea Seeds Journal.
It's a process of questioning, imagining, and going for walks through
my neighborhood of old trees.

For something as delicious as a gathering of some sort, especially created
by a woman for other women, I want the heart and soul of the event to
capture what women respond to when they're looking for something in
the context of a women's community: delight, laughter, understanding,
insight, support—no matter what the theme. If these are my goals for
outcome, my cultivation of those goals inherently require the very same
energy.

Before the event happens, I'm living and embodying my goals.

In addition to my Idea Seeding process: Meditation, sitting with Spirit, and a daily walk through nature, there have been three other significant *play in and with tools* that I've utilized at times for truly rooting more meaningful, successful, joyful gatherings:

Vision Boards, SoulCollage® Cards, and Candle Lighting with Prayer.

1) Vision Boards: The purpose of this board is to visually capture the desire of your dream so that you can literally look at it clearly—capture a vision of your goals and desires—and so that it can support your effort. Bringing an idea out of the swirling ether of possibilities and into your room as a manifested concept on a simple board will help you to take that idea to its next logical and more mature place of manifestation. Every time you look at your board, even just glance at it, it'll remind you of where you're going and its existence informs life of your intentions. I suggest viewing Jack Canfield's five-minute video on YouTube: How to Create a Vision Board.

2) SoulCollage®: This tool is more sophisticated than creating a vison board because it involves both an exploration of your dreaming and brainstorming, and adds a deepening process of *communicating* with the wisdom of the images you select. As chosen images come to represent the many aspects of self and soul, this process opens a door to the *why, when, what,* and *how* direction concerning those goals and desires. And because there are no words added to a SoulCollage® card (a 5x8 mat board or cue card that you paste images onto) your conversation with and from your soul can evolve in completely new directions over time—just as they would with a most wise and respected mentor. Once several cards are created for representing aspects self-exploration and the archetypes that live through you, you've got yourself a deck that can be used for consultation for a variety

of needs and dreams. I suggest visiting SoulCollage.com for simple step-by-step directions and resources galore.

3) Candle Lighting and Prayer: Simply and with enduring meaning, lighting a candle to reinforce an honoring, a desire, or a connection with Higher Power, has been a part of human ritual across millennia and world traditions. Decide your intention, write it down, plant your feet, light a candle, speak your written intention from your grounded core of being. This practice can be wonderfully powerful. Because each time you touch a match to a wick, not only do you practice something in the footsteps of every human before you who lit a candle with a prayer, but you bring the energy of "light" and everything it represents to the very thing you are holding in your heart right now, so that it can shine into the reality of your life and the world. Be prepared. Write it down. Everything you pray out loud as you light your candle is key; frame everything in positive terms. The confident energy you bring from your soul through your voice into this ritual will endow your effort with energy for the outcome you want.

If you choose to do any or all of these *play in and with tools,* you will essentially welcome the spirit of the goal into your ability to work with it by meeting it part way before carrying-on with it, together, toward the outcome.

Tools are most helpful for building anything; it's the *joy* in using them that captures the cultivation of a sacred space most effectively.

Even With Problem Solving, Unplug to Plug In

You have a desire to step into leadership, or to fine-tune your approach, and have planted some good seeds of all sorts. You are prepared—have weeded and tilled the soil.

Now those little seedlings need some specific things in order to truly establish roots, and grow. Two of them are time and space.

TIME AND SPACE.

If you need an excuse to extricate yourself from some over thinking and working, from lingering worries or a hyper-focus and longing around your plans and goals, this is it: Just as everything that grows needs room to germinate in order flourish, you and your plans do too.

My beloved mentor, Ken, captures it best:

You don't plant something and then pull it up by its roots everyday to see how it's growing.

I have always found his wisdom to be true true true.

Time and space are the next step in cultivating the success of your event.

When I'm working with new ideas for a workshop, retreat, support group, or keynote address, I set aside time daily to focus on it, but I let go of it at some point in my day, usually between 4 or 5pm. In my off hours, I'm really off duty. Unplugged from my "work" as much as possible.

This includes not worrying about it; not the details, not the theme, not my proficiency, and not attendees either. How do I do this? I become absorbed in something else entirely:

Exercise, time in nature, crafting, writing, family and friends and spiritual pursuits, T.V, movies, comedy, Pinterest, travel plans, dinner plans, haircut plans, yoga.

In your off hours, continuously thinking about the thing you've planted will smother it. And you. And probably your roommates, unfortunately. While you might be inclined to believe you're proving to yourself how much you're willing to work for your goal—deserve it even more—overworking will tie you up in *attachment to outcome* so deeply (discussed in Chapter 9) that you will make it impossible for your intuition to blossom in new creative ways that would serve your goals in the first place. Impossible for those seeds to expand in the dirt. Grow some hardy foundation.

Paradoxically, being "off" allows any internal constriction to relax so that brilliance can find its way in, and on. Be intentionally off duty, but don't resist inspiration when it pops in.

Einstein said that no problem can be solved from within the parameters of the problem. I have always loved that insight. It gives me the visual that a problem lives in a box (parameters), and that everything in that problem box is only about the problem (in that box).

So step aside, nothing to see here.

Not only does stepping aside provide some breathing room, some sunlight finally, it's actually an action toward a solution that wants to be realized and applied to the boxed in problem box.

Here's a neat example:

The Greek physicist/engineer/inventor/astronomer, Archimedes, had been tasked with solving a math problem for King Hiero who suspected his goldsmith of cheating him—substituting silver in place of pure gold in the royal crown.

As brilliant and swift a problem-solver as he was, in his uber-focused moments, Archemides could not for the life of him (and his reputation probably) solve the thing. Mathematics—it really can be so very frustrating (I'm told). Meanwhile, the King was waiting.

However, when Archemides stepped away from his problem box and into his bath, more than good hygiene was had. His body displacing the tub water provided his great revelation:

"Eureka!" he exclaimed jumping out of the bath, and ran down the street naked toward delivering his solution.

This is one pants-less version of the story, but the point about perspective is the same everywhere. When you least expect to realize an answer, is the very moment you are most open to finding one.

What could be more mundane than taking a bath?

Unplug a while for the true recharge; doing so will shake loose the resistance and obstacles to plentiful inspiration. This is as powerful as it is simple.

When you consider the simple things in your life, they likely provide the most grounding and balance for you. And then the bigger things rest on that.

I root for rooting.

(And for not pulling stuff up by the damn roots to examine them for viability everyday.)

Without the risk of public nudity, how do *you* make that kind of room in your life?

Like your gratitude and meditation practice, like your healthy boundaries practice, like knowing that your self-care ingredient lists are your friend, make a list of everything that inspires you. And relaxes you. Refer to it often. Practice it. Repeat.

Truly, it's all the life-lived hours and years that have strengthened your backbone enough to stand in your power when you answer the call to leadership. Every experience you've had, from stumbles and problems, even traumas, to successes, joys, and education, have been *the* very preparation path toward your wisdom and empowerment—if you want them to be. Add now, some specific intentional tools and practices to round out your ability to serve through leadership.

Remember to meet the sacred in and around yourself first. It will be contagious among those you serve (and among a bunch of people who don't know why they feel so good when they're around you!).

You got this.

Middle

Nourish Business Details:

This is a space that's clear, organized, empowered, driven.

Chapter 11

Business Ownership, Marketing and Fees

Recast your current problems into proactive goals.

~Suze Orman

U p to this point before your gathering, whatever the theme and venue, you've planted all your personal self-awareness and dreaming seeds that will give you the *umph* to make it all work. Now you'll feed those seeds in focused ways to grow your event into a fully formed outcome.

Nuts and bolts time.

Business Is a Good Thing to Claim

Whether you're a new facilitator or presenter, or a seasoned one, if you accept payment for your services, you're also a business owner. Don't demure, own it; it's a very good thing to be paid for your time and effort, and for the skill you yourself have paid for in training.

I know and rely on some general business strategies that fill my gatherings to capacity, and I know many other business owners in my field and in my region specifically, who also practice with integrity some of the same business habits.

Every advertising and marketing organization will tell you how vital it is to know your target "audience." In chapter 4 I discussed this in terms of opening the creative door for the needs and interests of your target population—designing a program that meets potential attendees where they are, where they need to be, and what *you* need and enjoy. Here we take it a step further, from knowing your target population, to focusing your inviting efforts.

Let's go:

In business, filling your events is largely about marketing; drawing your prospective participants to you. Because if you want your events to involve other people who will participate in the events you offer, they need some exposure to you—to know you exist.

Whether you intend to make a living at this, or merely hold a few workshops a year, your target population wants to know that what you offer is meeting a need they have. And once they know you, to continue to attend your events, they'll need some bit of sustained connection with you through marketing (marketing can include: E-mails, newsletters, snail mail, social media posts, calls, texts).

In other words, your target population is interested in a relationship with you. But in business, it's not entirely their responsibility to maintain it, especially not at first; it's yours.

When "Business and Marketing Aren't My Thing"

Many new facilitating leaders, and some who've been doing this awhile say, "But I don't like marketing, or the business part of this, it feels fake to have to sell myself. I don't like competing. Why do I have to do this? I hate it."

If this is you, cut it out right now.

You can market and advertise and accept appropriate monetary exchange from your participants as an extension of the celebration of your heart's work in this world, without the sales pitchy energy. And, if you hate "it", any part of it, you are creating a competing energy around your own work—dedicated efforts that you have worked so hard to birth. That competing grey gunky energy will turn people away.

Cut it out!

As a customer, especially as a participant of workshops and retreats, do *you* want to be involved with a facilitator who feels terrible about some behind-the-scenes aspect of the event you're attending?

You do not.

This is true for your clientele as well. How will they know? They won't know exactly what the "hating it" is, but they won't feel the spark of YES about you and your event all the way. And when you're marketing and advertising you want people to feel the YES, ALL THE WAY.

It's okay bubbalah, if your mindset and approach are a bit off, as they are for many, this is adjustable too.

Marketing by Taking up Appropriate Energetic Space

By "mindset and approach are a bit off", I don't mean that you're failing to elevate yourself enough especially next to your competitors. What I mean is that you should consider abandoning the temptation of the comparing mind. I want to encourage you here to clear the cobwebs of your own thinking about the value of what *you* are suitably offering. What are you suitably offering?

Sing it, Sister!

As your colleague, attendee, friend, mentor, mentee, I want to hear about it, and feel it. It'll be a delightful experience for me to experience *you* in your grounded excitement for the thing you want to lead. When you're certain that you *should* take up space in the world around you, that your skills and passions and intentions are worthy of your own life, you will feel certainty that they can serve others too. There are a group of people who will want your approach even in the midst of other similar offerings. You and the seekers will be a good fit.

But in order for others to benefit from your offerings, they have to be made aware that you feel confident about what you can do, and that what you offer has efficacy. If you feel that beyond your confidence you're "selling" yourself, it's possible you're working too hard, erecting a façade indeed. I want to reassure you that confidence and humility are a good pairing—façades aren't necessary.

Your potential attendees are also your customers; you want them to have confidence in what they are "buying." How are you with gracefully accepting a compliment by the way? This is excellent practice. Now partner with your own (developing or fine-tuning) skills, and market your events with a call to others to join you where you are. We're all in it together, after all.

Just be yourself. The very best version.

The Middle Ground Between Arrogance and Self-Effacement

There will need to be some information about you and your workshop somewhere and lots of where: flier postings, an article, a class description. Market on your website, on Facebook, on the venue's website, in emails, on a flier posted on a door in eye-shot of your <u>target population</u>.

(But do not, I repeat, do not waste money printing fliers and posting them all over town. All over town is *not* where your target population hangs out. Where is your target population? Clarify with yourself.)

You can not rely on word of mouth to fill your workshop vacancies. Hiding in your fear of sounding arrogant will derail your efforts. There's a big difference on the scale between arrogance and self-effacement. I won't ever attend an event if the facilitator is too humble or self-effacing. I don't have time for that—a facilitator who doesn't celebrate her own skills and passion is not for me. I predict boredom.

When customers predict boredom, or can't visualize themselves enjoying an event, there's no internal motivation to attend. And if you believe that an event fee is the number one killer of attendance and that a free-of-charge-class will "remove all the obstacles that prevent people from actually attending," I will help you see more clearly here:

Nay.

The truth is that when you offer something on a wave of joy and confidence, others will want in, no matter the cost. I notice all the time people who "can't afford" things that might be deemed basic, but amazingly find the funds to attend out of town events. We all make choices about what we want to do. Give your potential customers a reason to want to make your event the priority of the season. In this context, with your target population, own the business hat you wear. You can take it off at the end of the (business) day.

Registration and Tuition Fees

Along with running a business—where your participants are also your customers—if you want repeat attendance (returning customers), you must also be professional with clear boundaries that are free of guilt. This will inform the following necessities: setting tuition fees, collecting them, and defining a credit policy for missed attendance.

Why are these things connected with repeat attendance? Because they establish a clean exchange of energy between you and your customer.

You might even feel that your facilitation is your calling—that it's a deeply spiritual way to live your life. It's wonderful if that's true. However, others can take "ownership" of your offering when they have also given something of themselves in exchange for it. In a business exchange you are not requiring your attendee to give everything—not an eyeball, or even just an appendix. Rather, you are asking for a reasonable monetary exchange.

This exchange becomes a commitment on the part of your customer to show-up physically, emotionally, mentally, spiritually. Some energetic skin in the game (again, not actual skin). It's a commitment from both of you to bring your best. In the registration stage, it's an "impersonal" exchange, which is much cleaner because it's just a business contract between you and she, not an emotional one.

(I say "impersonal" because I'm referring to the principle of not taking this contractual exchange deeply to heart. You have something to offer, others want it, great, they should show their valuing of it with registration. If not, that's fine too. You can both move on.)

Haven't you valued something more when you've considered it carefully, worked for it and then paid for it? How do children learn to value things? The kid whose piggybank slowly grows to buy a bicycle is the kid who will not accidentally leave it on the curb overnight.

"Scholarship" Sliding-Fee Scale

Research the standard going rates in your region for similar events. Because you might feel that your calling to do this work in the world includes offering your skills to those who can't afford your full tuition, you might consider offering a percentage of your spots to sliding-scale customers.

I often do this. It serves both my customer and me very well because I would much rather have the attendee who truly wants to participate—who will contribute to the energy of the gathering in a wonderful way because she is eager to participate—than anyone else. And then, I don't spend any more energy than that on the idea of a sliding-scale/scholarship, or the customers who take me up on it. Those customers and full-paying customers are all the same to me. Meaning, I don't feel in any way that I am being "generous" by doing this, nor "feel sorry" for someone who doesn't have the means to pay the listed tuition. It's a clean energetic relationship.

A sliding-scale is also a calculated business decision: I want and *need* interested invested participants (customers) to attend—to elevate the event—and I want them from a diverse pool within my target population. I can offer this option and still meet my necessary business profit-margin goals—which justify what the event is worth based on the time and energy and money I've spent in order to offer the service that I've lovingly and professionally developed and shown up to facilitate.

What percentage of sliding-scale customers to accept at each event, and which sliding fees to charge, are also a matter of careful consideration. In line with typical regional fees for similar events, this answer will come from your calculating and figuring about how you'll afford supplies, venue fees and more. Even non-profits have to do this. My personal policy is: Don't undercharge, don't inflate. There's always a comfortable middle ground.

A typical small gathering that I coordinate myself is usually made up of 12-14 women. Depending on my personal growth goals for the event (how much I would value the energy contribution of attendees), and depending on the needs of the group I'm serving (what and how I'm being called to serve), and depending on expenses, I might offer one quarter to one half of available spots to sliding-scale customers. In a typical gathering, it's usually 2-4 women out of 13 who take me up on the sliding-fee.

Sometimes I decide ahead of time how many spots I'll designate for that option, sometimes I just flow with whatever's happening in terms of registration: If my event is 70% or 80% full early on, I can designate the remaining spots for sliding-fee customers. Or, if the event fills quickly with those customers first, I might designate the remaining spots to full paying customers. If I feel compelled to facilitate an event no matter the monetary costs or my own valuable time, I don't worry over the profit margin.

Testing Your Tuition Decisions, Whatever They Are

About all this "fees" business of business, my guidance is this:

1) <u>Collect the "data"</u>. Research and learn what works well for a variety of business owners. That's your data. Ask small business service professionals in your community about how it's worked out and *not* for them—what they've learned along the way. I find people are usually generous with their stories.

2) <u>Bounce things around with a confidant.</u> a) My husband is a good one but his schedule can be tight, I suggest talking to your own spouse. b) Or, seek a more objective bouncer. A few years ago, I trained in Martha Beck's Life Coaching Institute (now called Wayfinding Life Coach Training) and found it to be a terrific source of grounded support and direction that empowered people to intuit their own answers; I recommend a few sessions with a Martha Beck coach or another from a reputable training organization. c) Engage a powerful process like SoulCollage®[6] with it's journaling accompaniment, to help you tap into collective archetypal wisdom, as well as the inherent savvy of your own soul and mind.

3) <u>Sleep on it.</u> Again, research and fact finding missions are little nuggets of potential. After you've attended them, rest them. And you rest. After the data collection and bouncing-things-around stages, I like to sleep on big decisions for at least a week. Prayer fits in here too—candle accompaniment or not, send up a request for some perspective.

4) <u>Try it on, how does it feel in your gut?</u> Now that it's been rested (and wrestled out of your worried grip), germinated a little, been prayed over, how does it look and feel? Sit with it quietly so that you can *try it on* by playing with the following process

---

[6] www.SoulCollage®.com

(that I love from Martha Beck's training and use in a variety of personal and professional contexts):

Breathe and focus on the relaxation of your belly and heart. When you consider a decision, like charging a specific dollar amount for a workshop, how does it feel in those relaxed gut and heart spaces? Did you suddenly feel constriction? If so, it's too much girlfriend, dial it back a little to a lower tier dollar amount.

Or, did it feel comfortable and heart-and-belly fulfilled? Turn it up a notch with a higher tier dollar amount until you *feel* you've gone too far—again, constriction is more than a clue, it's an obvious *no*. A sensation of comfort, or heart warmth, is a *yes*.

Playing around frequently with this exercise (with trivial and important issues) will help you learn your own internal guidance sensations—the way your innate wisdom guides you into the *yes's* and the *no-don't-go-there-s*.

Guest Teaching and Adjunct

Guest teaching is a great way to make yourself visible to a population that might not have knowledge of you, or who have, but haven't felt motivated to try out your offerings.

At the end of your guest-gig, you should pass around a pad of paper that you've pre-printed to collect names, cell numbers, and emails. But first, announce that this is an optional collection of information. Give attendees the direction to sign it only if interested in receiving email invites about your next events. I like to do this in the final Q and A minutes of whatever I'm facilitating. The pad goes around while people ask questions.

I'm unattached to how many people sign. Again, being unattached, is not being "detached." I care, I just don't count on it, or dwell on the outcome one way or the other.

I really enjoy guest teaching. I like working with a passionate hosting organization or studio owner—there tends to be a lot of excitement in that because leadership facilitation along with our mutual interest in the subject are front and center. And I like being connected to other leaders who care about health and wellness. Many of them become friends.

You can research organizations, businesses, and venues in your field that feature guest facilitators. Start with your own community. This research involves your patronage of organizations, businesses, and venues. Where do you like to take a class? Look at what your library is offering. What your place of worship is offering. What your local extension office is offering. What that friendly looking yoga studio, or arts place, or integrative health gathering place is offering. What the healthy foods coop is offering. Avail yourself of their offerings. If you have a good experience there as a customer, introduce yourself to the manager. Establish a friendly relationship. Chat about your work and how it might resonate with their needs and the mission of their business. Ask if you can email some information about what you want to offer at their venue.

This means you should have a well edited informational one-pager at the ready on your computer, or a link to your website's informational page to send by the end of the next day. Don't wait longer than that to follow up, you don't want it to seem that your conversation and the potential of working together isn't a priority after all. You want to appear to be reliable and trustworthy. It begins with your timely follow-up.

And then, if you haven't heard back, it's important to follow-up again in a week, or ten days at the most. You might say something like:

Hello So and So, I enjoyed our chat about the possibility of my facilitation at your place, and I emailed you my information. I'm checking in to make sure it found its way to your inbox…

Guest Teaching Fees, Honesty and Negotiation

Here we are at fees again. Usually, when you're the guest workshop facilitator, you'll set the fee for attendees based on what the class should be worth, and then the hosting organization will advertise that fee, or upcharge it a little to cover their costs. I set my tuition fee based on the going rate in my field(s) for a similar event, for a similar number of hours, especially offered in my region.

And then there's a standard typical tuition split of 60/40 between guest facilitators and the hosting business. That is, 60% of the tuition collected is given to the facilitator, and 40% goes to the operating business whose responsibility it is to advertise, market, collect the fees, pay you on time, and provide the space. Sometimes, the split is 70/30 here, again in favor of the guest facilitator who is developing the workshop and leading all day.

These "standards" can shift; check on going trends in your region right now. But there can also be room here for friendly negotiation. If a hosting organization commonly pays a rate that's below what you value your service and experience to be worth, weigh what it's worth to have exposure to the hosting organization's population. But if you're shy about being honest with another business owner about your fees, consider that this is your issue, and no one else's (and here, again, consider booking a session with a coach to help you clear the cobwebs, because your business contacts want a clear, clean conversation with you about monetary exchange. Don't make them uncomfortable with your weirdness about being paid, whether it's below your fee, right on, or above. Be professional here. This is good business practice).

If the recruiting organization is one that I believe in and want to work with, my personal business policy includes negotiating with that organization some way to make it work within the parameters of what they can afford. So, I will usually ask if there's a way to work out additional funding such as opening the event to the greater public (beyond the group they are already planning to accommodate) and charging that group a small fee to attend, enough to make up the difference between my hourly rate and what the hosting business is initially offering.

If the answer is no, that they can't do that, and if it's worth it to me to agree to their terms and meet their specified needs, I'll do so happily and without reservation, and with no strings attached. If not, I'll say that I can't dedicate the time and effort for the fee offered at this time, but that I'd like to revisit a collaboration in the future if something changes on their end, or mine. I leave the door open for the potential of future collaboration and negotiation.

Intentionally Gifting Participation

There are at least five instances in which I offer completely free tuition to a participant.

1) To someone I don't know well, but just feel moved for some reason to offer a gift—maybe she's new in town. Or maybe I have the sense she'd bring so much to the gathering.

2) To someone I do know from another context of my life, but who hasn't attended this kind of event. It might be a thanks for something, or just a sisterhood gift—I might say to her, "I think you'd love this, here's the information. If you feel this event will resonate with you, please attend as my guest."

3) To a potential host. In this case I'd say, "Come as my guest and if you enjoy it and like the way I facilitate, consider hiring me to facilitate at your event, or training, or workshop, or retreat."

4) To a dedicated frequent-throughout-the-year, attendee, no strings attached. This is a business gift of appreciation that represents my heart-full gratitude for their patronage. An invitation to attend a gathering free of charge says, "thank you" for your dedication and support, and for showing up in the best way you can, every time you attend.

5) To a trustworthy frequent-throughout-the-year-attendee, in exchange for her help setting up, running the event, and closing shop. This is a great way to satisfy my need to NOT be burned out and frazzled by the time my participants show up. Plus, asking for and accepting assistance has established a deeper connection between my dedicated attendees and me. In case it's helpful to you, this is how the conversation often goes for me:

Me: Linda, I value your participation so much and could use your help. In exchange for free tuition, would you consider helping me set up (and close shop) for the next afternoon retreat on XYZ?

Linda*: Yes! Tell me more.*

Me: We'd meet 90 minutes before the start-time, arry bags from my car, set up the gathering space with chairs, set up the circle in the middle with flowers and chocolate and books etc.

It would help me if you'd stand at the registration table when people sign-in and collect any outstanding registrations (I'll give you a list), make sure people pick up name-tags, and then direct them to bring their journals and choose a seat. If I need assistance with something during our event, I'd call on you to help.

Cleaning up after will probably take 30 minutes with two of us. Does this sound like something you'd want to do?

Linda*: This arrangement works for me, thanks for thinking of me.*

Me: I'm grateful that you're game; knowing that I can count on your help will help me to not worry about details once I arrive to our venue. And, I'll look forward to spending extra time with you.

When to Show Up Completely Free of Charge

In the following contexts, when there are no funds to pay me, I consider my facilitation volunteer work. I like to volunteer.

Over the course of my life, I've volunteered at countless agencies and organizations, and all of them appreciated my time and effort, I'm sure. But there's something I love to spend my time doing most: facilitating physical, emotional, mental, and spiritual wellness.

So I volunteer from the place in myself—in my life—where I can give something free of charge, that I'm passionate about and that meets a need in my community and beyond.

Here are some contexts in which I've volunteered my services in recent years: cancer support groups, wellness conferences, unity rally, public schools and private and public colleges, community extension offices, on-line workshops for various hosts around the country, radio show, my religious community, and local social service agencies.

Now, back to you again:

Strategic Freebies and Being Prepared

When building your business, freebies are a great way to make yourself visible to the public, or to a specific target population. You can offer all kinds of little things to the public that give them a taste of your teaching style or themed presentation. However, strategic freebees should land in a different category from volunteerism; consider volunteerism to be a no-strings-attached arrangement where you're showing-up because you can contribute. (Though, volunteerism *can* sometimes garner some new paying clientele. Always carry contact cards with you—if someone is interested in your services, you've been gifted with an opportunity that you didn't have to work for. It's a gift you can be gracious in receiving).

But a strategic freebie, when you offer your facilitation without charge, is an intentional action oriented step that you take to make yourself more visible to your target population. Collecting participant contact information—email and cell phone number—is essential to your future livelihood. Always carry with you a way to record that contact information. The Notes function on my phone is my go-to.

It's always good when someone asks for your card—they'll carry home (or to work) a piece of your leadership energy—that's great, but don't rely on people contacting you. It's your job to follow up by reaching out shortly thereafter to invite them to an event, or to explore facilitating for their organization. If you're offering a freebie as guest on-line facilitator or blogger, make sure the hosting organization or site posts your contact information. It's your responsibility to ask for the contact information of those who participated.

Whether through volunteerism, a freebie offering, or through an offer to guest-facilitate, being prepared does not mean that you're being predatory, it means that you're being realistic about the fact that your specialty can benefit others, IF they want it. Being prepared means that you can *offer* your specialty without attachment to others taking you up on it. And it means that you'll move forward from there: Taking an action step, or, letting go of a daydream you've had involving that organization.

And, if people no longer want a business relationship with you, they can let you know. It's their responsibility to be clear about that, not yours to worry about. If you're a newsletter emailer, provide an opt out option.

Specific Freebies

Freebie offerings are popular on-line frequently now. You can offer a 30 minute or 60 minute on-line intro class, or a free phone consult and gather some new customers this way. I like it when facilitators post a brief expertise video about something they specialize in, but don't require me to sign up for a free anything after. I've contacted some that way.

And regionally, facilitating leaders can offer free try-us-out open-houses or brief workshops. These can work very well. Here again, when customers walk in, *your* collection of *their* contact data is essential. They are potential clientele. If you don't have a way to connect with them about future events, they won't know you're still in business.

If you offer a freebie gathering, and only a small percentage of those participants join you in the future to a tuition-fee gathering, celebrate that your strategy worked. A few new customers from every guest teaching spot or freebie-open-house will add up to a lot of new customers over the course of the year. Don't expect that everyone will be a returning customer, but be thrilled when they are!

Let your mindset rest in a place of integrity and clean, clear, boundaries where nothing is personal. The people who will most benefit from your beautiful offerings will attend your events frequently, and occasionally, and maybe only once. In every case however, you have done your business best and can rest at night with your integrity and your best efforts.

Chapter 12

Busy-Work Nuts, Berries, and Bolts

Everyday brings a choice: to practice stress or to practice peace.

~Joan Borysenko

Time Mapping

In leadership, details are your friends. They take your inspirations from airy thoughts and dreams, to the blooming of the specific goals planted in your Idea Seeds Journal. Those goals are meant to evolve from inspirations and dreams, to actual detailing about exactly how they'll look (how they'll play out) when they bloom on the actual day of your event once everyone has shown-up.

All together, it's the inspiration and the substance planning and follow through, that make up the actual program you're developing. Your attention to detail is the water to your seeded goals.

Time Mapping is a facilitation tool I never live without: The details of how I plan each time segment within an event, are essential for me as I make up a well thought out, mapped out schedule to define the parameters of the gathering. It's for my private use and reference while addressing my participants. It tells me when to say X and when to introduce Y.

Something magical can happen from this process. For me, mapping the time structure in my planning stage seems to open more inspiration—details fill themselves in. The Time Map becomes the gathering structure itself. This provides a lot of predictability, which gives me a lot of confidence that I'm ready.

Back to the Idea Seeds Journal:

Here's an Ayurvedic Health Retreat rough time-mapping example—but any theme or reason for gathering plugs into this.

(No one would see these notes on the day of the event, they're just for you to refer to and speak from, and to keep you cognizant of the time. I like to type them up in a size 14 font so that I can glance down easily at the parenthetical points without slowing down too obviously, because I like my presentation to be conversational in tone.)

Ayurvedic Health Retreat, Decemeber 4, 1:00-5:30PM

12:40-1:00:   Participants Arrive, Sign-In, Pick-up Name Tags, Settle-in.
1:00-1:25:   <u>Opening Circle</u>
- Housekeeping Details (thanks, venue info, bathrooms, make yourself at home).
- Agenda Plans (Explain: sitting and conversation will be no more than 90 minutes at a time. **Today will include: lecture & discussion, NIA dance, chit-chat, kitcheri, abhyanga, meditation, closing Circle**).
- <u>Participant Introductions</u> (say name, say where you're from, say one thing you love about winter).
- Self Intro (I'm passionate about facilitating groups, Ayurvedic lifestyle helps me stay balanced).
- Confidentiality (participants should agree with a nod *yes* that the stories of others shared at the gathering, stay confidential).

1:25-2:30:	<u>Theme</u>
	Ayurveda intro, and, self diagnostic Dosha questionnaire, Q & A
2:30-2:40:	Bathroom break and prepare for movement.
2:40-3:15:	NIA dance
3:15-3:45:	Water & bathroom break, kitcheri and snacks, choose the oil that smells best for abhyanga (L will pour into tiny cups and distribute to seats).
3:45-4:30:	Lead abhyanga and meditation
4:30-5:30:	Closing Cirlce: Ayurveda Q & A, and, any new self-discovery today? Articulate take-away-s (Pass or Play: what is one gem you'll take with you from this day?).

Notice my attention to time detail—it's important in the planning stage to allow the big picture to clarify. But during the event, I won't stick to it strictly because as much as I like predictability, I also like going with the flow of some detours that lead to unexpected adventures. As long as I'm close to time structure, I'm pleased. Creating it endows the program with support.

Before the mapping stage, I had a theme in mind but wasn't sure how I'd introduce it. Writing it out in my Idea Seeds Journal (or making a vision board or a new SoulCollage® card, or lighting a candle with a spoken prayer, see chapter 10), enables me to truly focus my goals. But once the time skeleton is written down at this stage, I can visually see how the time will flow within the workshop itself—what I'll have time to introduce and implement.

And then I fill-in as I go along. How I'll introduce the theme, and what I'll say about it in the time allotted crystalizes as I play with it—the time parameters hold the space for the meat of the teaching.

After hand writing the schedule this way in 20 minutes of brainstorming—including cross-outs and edits, I'm part way there for the final picture. For me, it's in the typing-up stage (in size 14 font), which I do within 24 hours, that makes me feel very secure with the plan and the way that I'll lead my group into the fullness of the teachings. I usually do some significant time and details editing at type-up time for a final filled in, clean, Time Mapped snap shot of my event.

This process has worked for me very well; figuring out *when* to say something and *how*, will also help you to *not* give away everything you know in one exhaustive sitting. This is very important and prevents overload for your participants.

Too Much Is Way Too Much

"Lisa, don't give all your wisdom away in one afternoon."

A dear mentor, J.P, said this to me years ago. It was invaluable guidance that became a bedrock support—integrated into my awareness about what my participants needed, what they could handle, and what they could digest and utilize from my teaching.

New facilitators often try to pack a little too much into one event: Too many concepts and too many tools.

Sometimes that can come from wanting to prove your validity as a leader. Sometimes from a lack of awareness about the right amount of information for one sit-down. Either way, participants can be overwhelmed by your generosity of information. Bite-sized curriculum is best.

Think of it this way, eating can be a deeply pleasurable experience when meals are spread out over the course of a day, a week, and a month. No one would feel well during or after eating a month's worth of meals all in one sitting.

The Time Map can help contain you and keep you from the Niagara Falls precipice of letting it ALL out—too much, too soon.

The Enchantment of Opening and Closing Circles

Returning attendees sometimes ask me why their experience in our Women's Circles feel different from other workshops and retreats they attend. They use words like: magical, transformative, warm, profoundly supportive, sisterly, joyful.

Before they ask, they tend to think it's the *way* I lead.

They're partly right. It is the way I lead (with care in the cultivation and facilitation stages and abiding by ethical standards to be in "right relationship" with participants), but it's specifically the energy of intention behind the elements I lead participants directly to—the elements that *they* come to engage in. That is the "different."

Here's the secret sauce from my perspective: I allot 30 minutes to opening circles, and 30-60 minutes to closing ones. The opening and closing features are a significant part of holding the sacred space container for participants to explore within, and then take out into their worlds.

Not everyone designs a gathering this way, and many foster transformative experiences without them, but I do if I can help it because I've found them to be part of my signature as a facilitating leader. I really, really like them and I like it when participants articulate their take-away-s before they depart. And so do my participants, returning and new.

The reason I carve out over an hour of the entire afternoon's gathering for these two elements combined is because they feel luscious to participants, especially because my participants attend my events as much for the camaraderie—the sisterhood tune up—as for the themes. What's articulated in the Women's Circle builds cohesion—which is good for participants and for me—and it helps them relax quickly.

1) **Cohesion From the Layered <u>Opening</u> Circle:**

When women arrive to my events and don't know one another but see that they'll be spending several hours with "strangers" in an intimate setting—exploring health and happiness—I want them to rest into a welcoming cohesive familiarity immediately. We sit down together in some form of circle, and from disparate experiences and lives, *individuals* become a *sisterhood* when they hear and feel others share themselves lightly. I say 'lightly' because in an opening Circle, sharing "your name, where you're from, and one thing you you're passionate about, or looking forward to", is light fare.

But it is an intentionally meaningful sharing (about how one engages in and with life, or sees beauty in the world, or is passionate about) rather than an ego-full sharing (about positions or titles that prove worth). And light-fare-meaningful is key to truly connecting with others, essentially bypassing a veneer of protective self coating connected to self worth.

And it's a doorway to connecting with self, too.

From his daily meditation newsletter, Fr. Richard Rohr, founder of the Center for Action and Contemplation, recently wrote: "Spiritual maturity is to become aware that we are not the persona (mask) we have been presenting to others."[7]

It really just takes practice to discern the truth of that and then the identify the safe contexts in which it's okay take it off. As a leader who is a sacred space cultivator and holder, it's enriching to have practiced authenticity with self and others—to first realize the great benefit in this—and then facilitate it for others in your gathering space.

Moreover, sharing what one "is looking forward to" or is "passionate about", allows participants to see each other lightly and deeply at the same time, and to see themselves—from diverse lives—in one another. There's ALWAYS yes nodding, laughter, and sighs generated in an energy of relaxation, happy

---

[7] Center for Action and Contemplation Newsletter, Sept. 13, 2019

anticipation (rather than nervous), and, a crucial awareness of support.

More than a sisterhood, participants become a group in a supportive therapeutic setting from the opening Circle design, and that group cohesion elevates the potential for participants to engage in a deeper personal experience while there.

Happens every single time.

Imagine after that, how easy it is for me to teach anything! My introduction to the theme of the day immediately follows and is received with the same cohesive joyful YES nods, YES sighs, and more laughter. It's a pleasure for me to spend time in that energy.

2) **Transformational Energy Dynamics:**

When I closed my private practice as an energy healer, what I knew was that I wanted to make more time to dwell in the lovely sisterhood space, both as a facilitator and as a woman who appreciates the companionability of quality time with other women—learning and growing, together. And I enjoy connecting people with people.

My intention therein is to make room for transformation to blossom within a group context. I don't promise transformation, but I do leave lots of room for its potential. For me, this is the he*art* of leadership in service.

Because the opening Circle practice is now an established "way in" toward those goals (for myself and those in my care) the opening 30 minutes is a ceremony that carries *us* along into the best I have to offer.

If I'm not feeling well for some reason, or am uncharacteristically nervous with a group, the energy of this opening (ceremonial)

Circle facilitation practice—now long grooved in my aura as a transformative tool—paves the way for me. Without a doubt, this tool elevates potential for the group beyond what I'm humanly capable of helping along from my "off" state that day.

3) **Cohesion From the Layered <u>Closing</u> Circle:**

Before they leave my gatherings, participants benefit sweetly and thoroughly from an opportunity to integrate what they've discovered and learned about themselves and one other. And, in a brief afternoon event, they might establish friendships here since support for one another has been building all afternoon. This is one reason I encourage participants to articulate their take-away-s.

That's about it. I encourage you to try various openings and closings to see what jives. Or, try out what I've described, or try something that you've experienced in a group, and let me know how it goes. I want to encourage you to play around with what works each time you facilitate until you find the right fit for your groove. Then, establish it as a reliable feature of your style. It will help you, and your participants, time and time again.

Even if your event is only 90 minutes long, and your participants are sitting all over the room, an opening and closing Circle can still be integrated in five minutes at the beginning and end. In this case, rather than going around the room systematically calling on everyone to participate, you could open the floor for general sharing based on the theme.

A quick opening Circle, if you're facilitating a fiction writing workshop to explore character development, might sound like this:

As we get this workshop rolling, let's begin with big characters and subtle characters in your own life. Think of someone you know, or think of a fictional character who intrigues you. Just call it out: What qualities of character intrigue you? Go...

Setting the energetic groundwork for a cohesive group energy—even through something as general as "characters who intrigue you"—not only gets the ball rolling, it invites participants into the theme and the next stage of the workshop. Then, you're not teaching *at*, but *with* participants. You're integrating their voices and presence into the space and involving them in discovering their own wisdom through the articulation of their own solutions. And inspiration of one another.

When participants speak up, they add their energy to the space, claim a place in it, and build the capacity of infinite creative possibility.

A brief closing Circle—even just 5 minutes—is the necessary book-end to the heart of the gathering. Most notably, it helps participants crystalize their intentions moving forward. Which, in my opinion is the most important part for an attendee.

If you are handing out feedback forms, leave 10-15 minutes at the end of the event for them to be filled in, but do it after the closing Circle.

(Find more on feedback-forms in chapter 19. Stay tuned, friends.)

Chapter 13

To Do's That Make It Possible for You to Do Less

Restore your attention or bring it to a new level by
dramatically slowing down whatever you're doing.

~Sharon Salzberg

Preparation and organization before an event will allow you to be grounded and present in the presence of it. Because of your preparation, everything you need at your fingertips in your gathering will be available and you won't be scrambling around looking for things. Plan to arrive early to set up the room, organize your teaching tools, and to calm the H down before your participants arrive.

It's important to be *the* calm participants want to see/feel/hear/experience when they walk in the door.

Bring Lists

Once I've typed-up my Time Mapped schedule, I'm very clear about the resources and supplies I'll need to support the programming I've filled in. Based on the sample Time Mapped schedule in Chapter 12, I make lists of needs that coincide with each time slot.

You might be surprised how meaningful it can be to gather up "stuff"—how much support those seemingly minor supplies offer to the success and joy of the program you're putting together. If your programming is the brick foundation of your event, your supplies are the mortar that can help you take it from a workshop or retreat, training or presentation, and elevate it to a sacred gathering. The mortar stuff keeps you organized and will be the tools your participants use for delving into personal exploration.

Those supplies are the tangibles of this special thing you've created—so they are special, sacred, because you will have endowed them by collecting them in a good and sacred way.

I typically list and bring the following. But just because I bring these things every time, doesn't mean I won't forget them on the day of the event. Again, a list is a friend:

My clip-board with:

- My Notes, Handouts, and Feedback Forms (if I'm using them).

- A time keeping device (phone or watch).

- Name tags (always, always).

- Back-jack chairs (if we're floor sitting).

- A portable table (if the venue is a yoga studio and doesn't keep a table).

- SoulCollage® supplies (if it's a SoulCollage® event).

- Yoga props (if necessary).

- Extra pens and paper (in case people forget theirs). (They will).

If I'm the host and facilitator, I might bring the following, no matter what the theme because they support many elements of my gathering:

A fruit bowl (little oranges, bananas, apples).

Chocolate (duh!).

A pretty cloth to set out uplifting books.

Hay House Inspiration Cards (one of my very favorite things to bring to EVERY event).

Rocks and or crystals.

Flowers, or a plant.

Think of what you've appreciated at the gatherings you've attended. Bring that stuff.

Advance Notice Advertising Invitations and Timing

It's important that potential attendees have plenty of advance notice about your event so that they can make it a priority over other things that'll compete for their time commitment.

And, advance notice (a personal invitation email) is a professional courtesy from you that implies you don't expect people to drop everything and attend your late-notice event.

Consistently, an emailed invitation with complete details—at least four weeks ahead of your local event—is appropriate. If I don't hear back from people, I email again a week later. If it's someone I know, I say something like:

Hello So and So,

I hope all is well in your world. I'm checking in here and wanting to make sure that my email to you last week made it to your inbox. I'm leading an afternoon retreat on xyz, and I think the theme, abc, would resonate with you. I'd love you to join me in the Women's Circle—you always contribute so much. Do you want to come spend the afternoon?

If it's someone I don't know well, I send a similar, but still personal, sounding note.

It's not "too much," and you're not bugging someone by expecting a response to your invitation of *yes, no,* or *maybe.*

And I put a lot of stock in the idea of a personal emailed note accompanying a link to the website description of the event—whether it's my website or the site of the organization hosting me. It's more personal to be personally personable. People feel more compelled to consider an event when you've extended your self.

Those who respond with a **yes**, receive a confirmation from me within 24 hours, and then receive an emailed reminder with what-to-bring details, a week before the gathering.

There are times with less notice when I'll contact dedicated attendees to say that I've had some last minute opening in my schedule and would like to host a gathering "next weekend." But most often, I give people at least four weeks notice for a day-long or half-day local event.

Pre-Registration and Event Confirmation

When I'm coordinating and facilitating, I like to know exactly how many people will attend so that I can properly prepare—not just with supplies, but with the energy of those attending. Because of this, my events require pre-registration with full tuition payment, and if I still have some openings close to the day of the event, I'll accept later registrations, too.

Pre-registration is important to me because I'm crafting the finer tunes of the program with attendees in mind—shaping the elements around *their* interests and needs. And if I don't know some attendees personally, having their names at least provides me an energetic feel for who they are.

And, pre-registration pushes a potential participant to commit to showing up after they've expressed interest.

Period.

As I dedicate hours and hours to program preparation, I'm not okay with wishy-washy commitments—a person is either attending (making the event and their participation a priority), or not. My preparations are a commitment; in this important exchange, an attendee's registration is theirs.

I think of it this way too: When I'm a participant in a workshop, I want the facilitator to count me in, count on me. It's a commitment that is also a courtesy. I'm a fan of decorum and the integrity of exchange in a relationship, including business ones.

If the event is a free offering, a participant's commitment to attend is still very important to me; again, dedicated hours of preparation for her benefit.

When you're the facilitator—offering a free of charge workshop—you'll rely even *more* on attendance commitment because you won't be recouping any funds in exchange for your effort.

Either way, not only is pre-registration a mutual exchange of respect for the service and your time offered, it's also a way to allow you to know that you won't have to scramble to fill the spot that someone verbally committed to, but wasn't serious about.

Be a Reliable and Direct Communicator

Whether pre-registration requires a monetary commitment or not, the action of pre-registering is another form of vital nourishment for the seeds you're trying to develop for your event.

Those seeds are meant to flourish into something more, to move into the next stage of growth for your gathering. You're designing something with your target population in mind, but without at very least the names of individuals for whom your event is designed, you are designing for an amorphous phantom population.

Without registration and assurance that people will show up, you're missing a vital part of that growth hormone.

If individuals don't respond to a reminder about your event, move on—no hard feelings—but you have work to do, baby, because you have an event whose success depends on the participation of a certain number of attendees. Again, a "critical mass" is necessary to help hold the sacred container of your gathering, and so that participants help each other, and so that the energy of needy participants is diluted among the cohort, and so that creative healing potential can thrive.

Am I right?

Once a participant mails-in her registration check, or pays you on-line at the link you've provided, send her a confirmation Email, and do it in a timely way—within 24 hours. This is part of your organized approach to a professional relationship here. Don't leave her guessing, or assuming that she's in. And include in this The-What-to-Bring details which you will send again a week before your event.

It's in your best interest to take a little bit of time for the reminder Email because YOU want people to show up (and show up on time), but also, your week-before-reminder builds more excitement and joy among your participants about the upcoming gathering.

When I'm communicating with my own participants, my e-confirmations are brief and always begin with: "I'm looking forward to our Gathering, I know you'll enjoy our day together."

And they always contain a reminder of the following, again:

1) The name of the event. The day, time, and location.

2) A what to bring list: journal and pen, water bottle, comfortable clothing, and what ever supplies are integrated with the theme (*what to expect details* about the event would have been included in the initial confirmation email).

3) A reminder that I'll begin promptly at X:00pm, and (if it's a small gathering) to arrive 10 to 20 minutes before our start time, to "sign-in and settle-in." At events that require more stringent adherence to a time schedule with contact hours, like a training of some sort, I ask participants to arrive 30 to 90 minutes before the event.

4) My cell # in case of unexpected late cancellation, which I specifically ask to be alerted to.

If all of this preparation on the To Do List seems like a lot of work, I can assure you that after doing it twice, it will feel more intuitive and less burdensome. And you can just cut and paste from your documents.

I really like preparing for an event; there's a great joyful feeling connected with preparation now.

Like learning a new instrument, it just takes a bit of practice before truly enjoying it.

Chapter 14

It's True That Size Matters (But Not Always)

The little things? The little moments? They aren't little.

~Jon Kabat-Zinn

Opportunity No Matter What

B e clear with yourself about your goals, aim for full capacity attendance, and work toward your goal.

Again here, why are attendance numbers relevant in a conversation about creating sacred space? It's relevant because the number of people who contribute to that space matter. Those who attend are endowers of the space you aim to create. Depending on the type of gathering, the variety of people among your group might matter, too. In most therapeutic settings, the more life experience and diversity and ethnicity and life focus among attendees, the (much) better support for your goal.

Based on the venue parameters and the way I like to facilitate my self-coordinated local retreats and supports groups, there are a certain number of people I prefer for small gatherings: 10-14 women in a group are about right for my type of programming goals, and for group synergy, typically. 12 or 13 tend to show up. Just right. When I'm recruited, the groups are larger, sometimes by hundreds, and, co-ed. Also just right.

It's taken me some time (through established venues that I now consider "home") to realize my preferences in each context. You will figure out your preferred size in preferred venues within the current chapter of your leadership and facilitation. And, your preferences will likely change over time.

What's more, if you consider yourself a facilitator who is co-creating a sacred space *with* the Higher Powers of the Universe, and *with* those real live humans who show-up, your conscious care about *who* and *how many*, matters as well. A critical mass, even for a small group is necessary for your particular offering, and you get to decide those parameters.

By the same co-creation token, try to avoid canceling an event due to low numbers; "low turn out" events are not only your opportunity to learn, practice and grow, it might be a *calling* to work with a small group for a change. A calling to something meaningful that you wouldn't have known to design of your own accord. I know of many celebrities and performers who work out new material in small venues before booking bigger ones. Also, sometimes an unexpected turn of events is a sacred unfolding—the meaning making sense later in retrospect.

This might be especially true if you're an experienced facilitator. A low turn-out might be a means to meet your competent curriculum in a brand new way: see it with fresh eyes and adjust it.

How Registrations Give You an All-Systems-Go-Ahead

About two weeks before a small local event (10 days maximum), once I've collected registration fees for at least 50% of my capacity goal, I can relax knowing that my event is a GO, and that the final registrations will roll right on in. If it's a free event, registration *names* are my GO.

It's often around the 14th day mark (before my gathering) that remaining participants commit to half-day or full-day gatherings, probably because generally, they're better acquainted with their plans. But also at this time, the increasing registration momentum happens because there's been an energy created by initial registrants that actually enhances the advertised event for me. In other words, registrants get the ball rolling for others considering registration. Even though they might not know one another.

Everything in the Universe is energy and momentum, your event included.

So, it really is in your best coordinating interest to be clear about your goals, and then assertive in your marketing long before the 14th day mark.

Work for it, and it will work for you. And then you can relax.

Dr. Phil Says We Should Teach People How to Treat Us

The 14th day mark *paid registration* goal for 50% of my participants is also a boundary that I intentionally schedule. This sets up an energy around my registration process that participants abide by even though they may not be consciously aware of my boundary. It says to people that I am organized, thoughtful, and expectant.

Eventually, your "regulars", who know how magical and transformative your events are, will register immediately, 4-6 weeks before your local event, out of concern that spots will sell out before they can register. Again, your intention, preferences and boundaries usher in what it is that you want, and this applies to your registration policy as well.

(For larger local events where venue fees are pricy, and for out-of-town gatherings where lodging fees are necessary and where a minimum number of participants is required to make it worth it financially for you, half of your registration fees should be collected much sooner: about 10-12 weeks ahead of your event since you have to actually pick up your life and travel to a teaching destination.)

Some coordinators offer early-bird discount deadlines to ensure registration in a timely way. This works very well because saving a little money is a big incentive for registrants.

Cancel, Break Even, Low Attendance

It's at this time, the 14th day mark before your local event, that you want to assess whether you should in fact move forward with your scheduled gathering. If, despite your marketing and advertising effort over the previous weeks, you have only one registrant, consider rescheduling. But if you decide that you *will* facilitate no matter what—most likely not meeting your full capacity goal as the days roll toward your gathering, be at peace with not meeting your original goal. Be accepting of it as you continue preparations.

In my early years, financially breaking even or making a small profit wasn't a measure of success for me. But it should have been. Breaking even is a triumph at first—and a sign that you're truly on the right track.

I can see today, looking backward, how valuable beyond the money were those small gatherings to my budding destiny as a leader and facilitator. It's easy *now* to connect the dots of how I became happy with my career and business goals. You can relate to hindsight I'm sure, from a variety of areas in your life. It can be difficult to have faith when you can't connect the dots ahead of you, or around you in the moment. It's only in retrospect that you can see the whole picture.

But that is what's required. Your spirituality and your faith in a desired outcome, and your faith in yourself, can, really, can, really, really can (!), carry you right into all that good career/business business, eventually.

My first self-coordinated Mexico retreat was a break-even experience. Out of eight participants from all over the U.S and Canada (which in itself should have been notably more celebratory for me), two were my teaching partners, one my sister, one my best friend. And, I waived the registration fee for one attendee from my home town in exchange for future advertising in her community news circular. That meant I had three paid participants altogether.

At the time, it felt like failure. Those three tuition payments just about covered my travel expenses, my own retreat lodging, my sister's and best friend's, and the cost of supplies for the program I led. But I just could not see what a gift I had been given in all that. Breaking even on a first foreign retreat! Success!

Here's why:

1. A small group is manageable for a newbie.

2. Most of that group—people I knew—were people invested in making the retreat (and me) a success. They invested in me. That investment paid confidence dividends during and after our gathering.

3. While I didn't make a financial profit, I spent a week at the ocean eating excellent food and enjoying the company of other women I loved and at least really liked, all while upgrading my facilitation skills. I left my regular predictable life at home and set off on a new adventure.

It was a quality foundational experience. A skills profit that I owe my heart to. I was a fool, too stuck in my head about some arbitrary measure of success related to size and income, to enjoy it fully at the time. Because I was chasing "success," I wasted the full presence of my psyche and the deeper blessings of appreciation that I could have enjoyed.

If you are a new coordinating facilitator, putting a lot of unnecessary attendance-numbers pressure on yourself, cut it out. You don't yet know how valuable this learning stage is—though you'll eventually see it. Try to be with what *is* without the flagellation of disappointment. You don't know what it means thus far. And, be sure, feelings of disappointment delay the abundance that is coming your way. Or at least trying to, because disappointment is an opposite energy to abundance energy. Which energy do you want to feed?

You have a choice.

So, get clear about what you want while being open to what comes. My two-week registration boundary with 50% of my desired group size (for purposely small-ish local events) emerged after I built my local business base. When first starting out, you're testing your own boundaries as well as others'. I figured out what worked for me through trial and error, and found this boundary to be comfortable and reliable.

And I can promise you again here that it's a good thing to start small (between eight and ten including you) and to *grow into* the sweet spot of your desired participation numbers and financial goals. How do you know what fits unless you try on a few sizes?

Plus, it's a much better success story to say that you "paid your dues" and "started out small" and "grew your business" alongside your set of skills.

Disappointment Dissolution

If, two weeks before your small group event, you've not met your pre-registration attendance goal but you resolve to move forward knowing that you might have a very low turn out, it's vital that you put away your disappointment. Feel it for an hour if you need to. Cry on someone's shoulder. Journal. Talk it out. But then señora, if you decide to move forward, you must do so with a sunny disposition. It will not serve you to feel badly, and it will not serve the three registrants who do show up, who are putting themselves in your hands.

If, after the first year as a facilitator (where you've been trying to make yourself visible in your community by offering your leadership in a variety of ways: guest teaching, free events, social media), you're still not meeting your desired goals for attendance at your events, seize the freedom to re-evaluate those goals, and to examine what the problem is. The first section of this book is chalk full of solid foundational elements to consider. There is a way for you to be successful—have all your facilitation dreams come true—it may be that your approach could use fine-tuning and some support. Or change in direction.

Last Minute Cancellations and Cancelling Your Event

There are times when, infrequent but they do happen to me still, that 25-50% of my small group event, committed pre-registered paid-attendees, drop out last minute. Especially for intimate Circles of 10-14 people, this is alarming. But, because I like to take the long view—that there might be some important dynamic at play here beyond my responsibility to mess with—an unusual drop out rate like this gets my attention in a "that's interesting" way.

The key word here: Unusual.

Generally, as the event holder of local gatherings, I just don't believe in cancellation unless I can give at least ten days notice to those who *have* registered, because I feel it's unfair to cancel them last minute. And business wise, I would much rather be associated with an intimate gathering experience—as a very small group facilitator—than as a canceller. Small and intimate can be very rich.

Yes, when attendance numbers are occasionally low, it does mean you might have to rework your curriculum plans to suit, but flexibility is doable. Boundaries don't have to be concrete walls. And again, based on your goals, financial included, if low attendance is a consistent circumstance you'll need to examine why. And do so while practicing self-compassion. When my attendance numbers are low, I check my marketing strategies, and most importantly, my own pervasive general day-to-day energy.

Growing your own Light as you lean into self correction or course correction, in turn influences the people of your external world in the healthiest of ways. As your beacon shines consistently, those you're ready for, with more Light, will find you.

Lean Into Learning and Surrender

However, let's revisit paradox again here: Goals, analysis and adjustments alongside "co-creation" with Higher Power, The Grand Poobah, Great Enchilada in The Sky. The Powers That Be.

Trying to align personal goals with what Spirit would have you do can be confusing. It's true that none of it is very clear cut.

As we say in Kentucky: *Bless your heart*. Bless mine, thank you very much.

If you are a facilitator who believes in creating sacred spaces for individuals to enter a group dynamic in which potentially transformative inner work can be realized, you must also live a mindset that surrenders to the mystery of why things happen the way they do when circumstances change. If your objective is to co-create with Higher Power in your life—in your desires and in your professional events—you must be in acceptance about the turn of events when you are disappointed and dissatisfied, as much as when you're delighted and satisfied.

Good happens, shit happens, mystery happens. And change too. It's all life and it's all fair.

I want to suggest *going with it* rather than resisting reality. Personally, I really like the feeling of surrender. Many people expect vulnerability in that, but I can promise that surrender can feel like a place to rest knowing that much greater forces than average-human-big-ego-me are the ropes and pulleys of the whole thing. Whose to say that your general and specific "for the greatest good" prayers aren't being precisely answered by an unusual turn of events?

But I don't mean that you allow yourself to be blown around untethered by the "random" winds and whims of change. I mean, be consciously, spiritually awake to what is happening, and then use your best logical intelligence to make new decisions.

Last year, nearly 14 years into my career as a facilitator, I offered to lead a workshop for free for a group of health service professionals in my community. I was motivated by appreciation for this population as well as by potential entrée with them to offer my workshop facilitation on an on-going basis. I predicted some future reliable income opportunities with this group. And I thought we'd find mutual cheer for our city, considering I'm also a service professional. Thought they'd be my "peops."

I was received by the organizer with appreciation and excitement for my offer to lead the free workshop at their regular meeting. She told me that about a dozen people attend the monthly gathering where I would facilitate. Two people showed up. One was the organizer, and the other, a member of the group who didn't read the email about that week's meeting focus, became hostile about the theme I brought to facilitate.

I know you feel me. Yes, cringe.

For half the group in attendance that night, the *Preventing Burnout and Filling Your Personal Well (Being) Workshop* did not resonate, despite the obvious truth that my title held a <u>reservoir</u> of promise. (I'm hilarious, people).

This hostility was disturbing as well as humorously ironic considering it was a health professional whose job it is to help people maintain personal mental health. Though, in her service-professional defense, it's very possible that she was struggling with something in her life and was simply not in the mood for personal exploration that night. She expected a meeting and ended up at a feel-good personal discovery workshop. Most people don't like an unexpected well-being bomb.

Either way for me, it was difficult. We were absent the critical mass to dilute the polluted energy. However, as the leader facilitating a "group" of two people (half of whom sent flaming energetic arrows my way) I knew I'd be testing my metal. And that awareness gave me room to experiment with my skills and the situation we were all in. Though I'm sure none of the hostility was personal, I *was* on the receiving end of it.

So, I got out of the way. An arrow has less chance of landing on yuh, if you're not wearin' a bulls-eye. I simply let it be (and let her be) and got on with my facilitation not expecting her to contribute.

I stayed in that situation because the other participant valued the process deeply and expressed that she'd been "hungry for this." And because I wasn't taking to heart the "negative energy" in the room but rather, felt curious about how I could maintain equanimity under those circumstances. I stayed because there was something in it for me too.

Another option would have been to call out the belligerent elephant in the room and address it—and provide an out for it. Something like this:

So and So, you said earlier that you hadn't read the email about this workshop embedded in your monthly meeting. It seems you're caught in a difficult situation here because clearly you don't want to engage with this workshop process right now. I want to offer you the option of heading out—no hard feelings at all—and I'll stay to offer Other So and So a private session. If you do stay for the remaining hour, these are my typical expectations for dyad participation: XYZ......

Now, what do you want to do?

With so many interesting dynamics (including me with myself) what a divinely designed gathering. For several reasons. That day, not only did I notice my own growth and ability to play in the go-with-the-flow-ness of events, but also, with just two attendees I got my "potential entrée with that community" answer:

NO WAY.

The Powers That Be were being droll specifically about the direction I should take. Legitimate SNAFU reasons aside, health service professionals who resist professional health resources are not my cup of tea. Ever. And then, it was the hostility cherry on top that provided more clarity about the truth that I'd be wasting my time wanting to work consistently within this resource network, no matter the reasons for poor turnout.

Great Enchilada in the Sky knows to send me witty signs I can recognize easily and chuckle over. Message received.

What's even more, as if that message wasn't valuable enough, the learning (and play) inherent in that strange facilitation experience was very good for me:

Since there were only two attendees, I needed to improvise the curriculum on the spot. With a good outward attitude, I will add. The practice of *looking* unflustered really does tamp down the internal fluster. *Never let them see you sweat,* is a good strategy for everyone involved, especially your own wired for fight-flight adrenals. In the moments of that experience, I learned about my ability to remain outwardly graceful when under stress in the presence of overt negative vibes—obvious signs that my regular meditation practice was rewarding me.

Well, who doesn't benefit from that training? Professional circumstances aside, I'm sure all of us have at least one challenging family member. Or five.

If you can remain calm under pressure with strangers, you've strengthened a muscle that will save you from evisceration from people who really know how to push your buttons over turkey at Thanksgiving. And later in an important professional meeting where your skills in diplomacy will help you get what you need and want.

And really, again and again, when improvisation is exactly what's needed from you as a leader, in any context.

From Surrender to Upgrades

Here's how that weird improvisation training served the evolution of my leadership—what it propelled me toward instead of just away from:

A year later while out of town, I attended a gathering where a brief guided meditation was spontaneously added to the schedule. It was added because during the course of the event I had shared a personal detail about the benefits of my regular meditation practice. Then and there, the facilitator asked if I'd mind leading his assembled group in a meditation before departing. Everything in me felt YES to that request, even though I had nothing "prepared".

Turns out I had in fact prepared in the most important sense. The grace I needed to hone, a year earlier under the pressure of a poor turn-out with a side of hostility, was the very same grace I'd need under the pressure of a spontaneous, unpredicted, call to leadership with a great turn-out.

Pressure is what creates a diamond.

At the end of the day, even if you're a business-owner facilitating-leader who relies on income projection, there needs to be a certain amount of surrender in your projections. It's most helpful when analyzing circumstances, to notice how things look and feel in present time. Not merely how they looked and felt originally. And then look in the direction that has the most light surrounding it. Or, as in my case, cheer.

Be that leader. If I can be, I know you can.

Go Time!

Shoots and Blooms:

This is a space that's prepared, confident, attuned, qualified.

Chapter 15

Bring the Sacred Space With You When You Arrive

Sometimes your joy is the source of your smile, but sometimes your smile can be the source of your joy.

~Thich Nhat Hanh

Be Your Own Programming Beneficiary

All your lists are checked: Your theme ready, your attendees registered, your healthy boundaries examined and updated, you feel the extent of the GO, and, your supplies gathered. All your busy work is complete; now it's time to revisit and dwell in your original inspiration for the gathering.

Begin by engaging again with the tools of the theme you plan to facilitate. That's right, sit down and play around with them.

If it's a writing class, pull out your own writing notebook and practice the thing you'll direct attendees to practice with. If it's a support group or self-awareness gathering of any sort, journal your heart out with the theme you'll introduce to your group. A SoulCollage® event? Make cards and work with the journaling prompts again. If it's a movement or yoga class, physically experiment with the movements or the asana again. An art class? A mountain hike? A key-note address? You get it.

Become the student of your own program.

But chiefly, be the first beneficiary of what you've created so far for your event. Be your own attendee. You're not meant merely to communicate the subject; it's intended *for you* to practice first of all, again and again. Be your own walking, breathing, billboard of success with the subject matter and tools you're offering.

The creation of the program that was just a little bud of possibility in your Idea Seeds Journal is now a living program. But as a student of life—as a sacred space creator and cultivator—you must feel it in your marrow and practice it before presenting it.

You can facilitate a program without doing this of course, but you're reading this book because you're interested in elevating your events from get-togethers to sacred space gatherings. For this to happen, the teachings that come through you have to travel from your heart and head and journal and handouts, into your reality of *doing* and engaging *with* and *being*, before you offer it to participants later.

This again, is the very art in the h*art* of your leadership.

As you do this—benefit first—you'll carry the benefits of your cultivated program vibrantly in your energy field. Your attendees will benefit from the fullness of your creation before you teach a word of the curriculum.

Personally, I feel a solidity and love for the subjects and tools I facilitate. They're vital health lifestyle elements in my own daily life. And though it sounds corny, I would say that I'm truly *in love* with the subject matter before I teach it. Because some of the material requires a review before a training, I get to fall in love all over again, often.

If corny is wrong, I don't want to be right.

I go back into the original wisdom teachings for other reasons too: To re-grasp my own understanding of the history and its evolution, and to review again how I'll present it.

Yes, I do this even though I've taught some of those subjects dozens and dozens and dozens of times, for a decade.

This intensive review of the subjects I facilitate is more than review, it's several things:

1) A re-engagement with the spirit of the original teachings, now sacred in nature. As I teach, I feel responsible for doing them justice.

2) It's a re-ignition and fulfillment of my passion for the subject, and a reminder of how I felt when I was first introduced to it years before—and how it grows in me now.

3) It's a re-invigoration of the excitement of learning the subject matter—exactly what I want my participants to feel.

In your first facilitation (and second, and more) you don't ever need to be perfect or hold yourself up to some standard you fear you'll never reach. Just being fulfilled by, in love with, and educated in your subject matter can make you a compelling facilitator of it when you walk into the room.

That fulfillment, love, and working knowledge, roll out the red carpet ahead of you. A carpet you have only to tread upon into the material you're facilitating, into the open and willing hearts and minds of your participants. Right into the sacred space that you will teach *from*.

If you don't at least like your subject a lot, don't teach it. Decide to explore it privately, or retrain in it again, but don't try to teach it without some heartened investment in it, it won't catch. Your students won't love you more for it.

And that would not be good for business. Because after all, a sacred space is sustained through pleasure. Which *is* good for business.

In a yoga teacher training I facilitated once, a self-declared Christian student asked me if the Vedic teachings of human bio-energetic field theory is "witchcraft or evil." This question came after two hours of lecture that included NASA published science and experiential processes ((pranayama (breathing), asana (postures), and mindful restorative relaxation)). Living in a heavily fundamentalist region, I recognized in this question the familiar pervasive accusation and fear of "evil" related to anything outside the parameters of the Christianity she'd been fed. It seemed half sincere, half accusing. But because I stand solidly on the foundation of those venerable teachings—am both a beneficiary and messenger of them—I stand with great confidence in them. I didn't make them up; they're historical treasures for us in modern times. This confidence has helped me to not take accusations or student fears personally.

From Challenge, Again, More Growth for You. Also, Neutrality.

After witchcraft question day, I felt again as I often do, that articulated questions live at the center of growth. And the even better news here is that your "reality" as a facilitator—with the principles you're teaching— might come to influence the reality your attendees live in eventually.

The teaching and learning space that you share, whatever the venue or theme, is exactly where you are creating a new shared reality. This is your sacred intersection with other. Your compassionate neutral influence might make a big difference in someone's life even if you never see each other again. Maybe you're the only worldly, conscious person they've ever had a personal conversation with. What a (non-proselytizing) gift you might be.

While you can't really "control" what happens in the environment or gathering space outside you (as you know from the benefits of meditation lecture), surely you can respond to it. You CAN influence it. Affect it. Contribute to it. Help it. Calm it. Shine some big Light into that very intersection between you and other.

That is holy ground, indeed.

But it is also neutral ground. Because you should not be attached to outcome (as you know from the healthy boundaries lecture here-in). You might become attached, but should *not* be.

Yes, <u>that</u> again. And since, as a leader and facilitator of healing, you're not in the business of selling anything—or convincing anyone of anything—you can simply bring it, offer it, and lovingly leave it there as a take-it or leave-it.

Indeed, that is neutrality inherent in the holy ground.

As a frequent student myself, I'm turned off immediately when a facilitator tries hard to convince me of anything. I don't like that crossed boundary. I don't like the pressure, and I don't like the way that facilitator's identity is tied up in my acceptance of the teaching. Yuck.

If you're questioning this neutrality thing, think of it this way:

When you throw a party and prepare a buffet of options, you are offering options, but you're not standing over your guests and assessing their hunger or interest in them.

There are all kinds of reasons that some people try everything and love everything at a party, and all kinds of reasons they hardly eat a bite. Likely, you as the party host will let them be *how* and *who* they are in relationship to the food you set out. This allows you to be exactly *how* and *who* you are in your own party-thriving-dining-room. It's best that you remain in charge of what you want to offer, and it's best that your guests remain in charge of what they want to consume and digest.

Together, party context or other, we can all be who we are. Everyone gets to decide what and how we'll try things in every setting we walk into. Including learning spaces.

Aim to be effective and to influence, not to convince, sell, rescue, or change.

Love Bomb the Space Ahead of Time

In addition to your own sacred-space-facilitator-preparation in all the ways discussed up to now, sending some big joyful energy ahead to your venue provides your very self with an extra dose of support structure. This gives you the best chance of *meeting participants where they are,* and gives you the best chance of affecting them most constructively.

Here's how to do so:

Envision yourself within the venue that will contain you and all the teachings you will bring. Envision the participants and the venue itself (even if you don't know the participants or venue). Know that your angels and the angels of attendees, and the Spirit Guides of the subject matter, and the angels of the venue—the Manitou of the place—are on stand-by to help per your request. Feel into your heart and ask for assistance from the stand-by team in blessing the venue and those who will attend. Envision yourself, the people, and the space within the venue filling up with radiant, loving, joyful Light. Envision yourself within the venue radiating the Light you are supported by. It's that easy. And effective.

Even when I can rest assured that my "audience" will trust me (because I know all the participants specifically), I usually send big happy Light filled energy ahead to the space before I get there. It provides extra support for me to maintain equanimity no matter what happens once I take up brief residence there.

This can even be done for on-line live workshops before they begin where participants are spread out all over the place, and where the computer or audio space you enter is more space-y and less defined-y.

Grounding and Breathing

I used to be flighty and "ungrounded" in general. I'd sprain my ankle on the regular. Say the wrong thing at the wrong time. Find my anxiety unmanageable. None of it great for leadership roles.

Again, who you are in your personal life is who you are in your professional one. As a leader, what you facilitate should be grounded in well founded subjects and valid tools. But first, you must be grounded in order to facilitate them.

"Getting grounded" is a technique, and a mindset, that will help you keep your head on straight and access your higher acumen. Lead from it. A grounded individual is an emotionally intelligent one who can soar with inspiration <u>while</u> maintaining a level head, *two feet on the ground.*

Like the benefits of meditation which calms the reactivity of limbic fight-flight wiring, *grounding* serves further to embody you *within* your physiology. It establishes your being WITH your body in present-tense rootedness. Being *beside yourself with worry,* is a real thing. Being *an air-head* is too. When you want *all your wits about you,* it's grounding that helps make it happen.

When you intentionally practice grounding techniques, you're tuning into the benefits of Earth's bio-energetic field, which sustains every living thing on our planet including the cells of your body. Essentially, we are all being breathed *by* Earth without thinking about it. But just as there's a difference between your faucet turned low to produce a trickle of water, and your faucet turned all the way to produce a forceful steady flow, your attention and intention to fill yourself with Earth energy will yield to you a quantity of available energetic sustenance to power you. Because you ARE energy.[8]

---

[8] For an understanding of the human bio-energy field and our cellular connection with the element of Earth, I recommend Rev. Rosalyn Bruyere's, *Wheel's of Light*; Carolyn Myss's, *Anatomy of the Spirit*; Dr. Manisha Kshirsagar's, *Ayurveda: A Quick Reference Handbook*; and, Gary Zukav's, *Dancing Wu Li Masters*

Just like your electric car needs to be plugged into a source of electricity, your electrically-wired body needs it too—replenishment.

Trees and their rooting systems make excellent symbolic and literal examples for us humans to emulate here: They have the potential to live long healthy lives taking up as much space as they need to fulfill their destinies, their limbs are graceful with movement as long as their roots are firmly established, and, they can even grow up through cracks in a sidewalk. They do all this by rooting first, by making a significant earthy foundation for themselves First Of All. And comparable to how mammals inhale air into lungs, trees engage in a continuous respiration process.

Under all manner of challenging circumstance, if trees can, you can. We're all a part of the same dynamic non-local intelligence creates worlds and sustains them. Us. Grounding and breathing are two most natural types of medicine for our human species. They are found in every wisdom tradition across the globe—good medicine in every single bag of tricks.

Whether we're talking about personal life or professional, a grounding habit will provide you more than *a leg to stand on*, it'll ensure you have two.

(Even when *the rug is pulled out from under you*.)

Try it:

- Sitting or standing upright, feet flat on the floor, feel yourself. All of you, your feet and scalp and everything in between. Whether you're outside, or on the tenth floor of a building or in a plane, breathe deeply and feel your feet.

- As you inhale and exhale slowly, let your feet sink into the floor like a tree growing roots down into the ground. You'll notice more sensation in your feet as you "sink them" and as your breath-cycles progress because sinking = synching. People report tingling, warmth, or heaviness in their feet and legs after a minute or two of this focused practice. I feel it almost immediately after decades of practice. If you're sitting on the floor, it'll be your rear-end feeling the feels.

- Each inhale "pulls up" energy (through your foundational 1st chakra center)[9] and allows you to ground with more solidity and flexibility. More balance. Again, turning on your faucet full tilt, this energy travels up your feet and legs, then through your spine and replenishes all the cells and organs it travels through—arms and hands too. Once energy reaches the top of your top, it fountains out the crown of your head (your 7th chakra center).

- A nice side affect often reported: "I feel solidly rooted but light at the same time."

During my most chaotic and taxing chaplaincy rotations when I was on-call in the midst of an overnight shift—paged all over the hospital from the ICU to Emergency Room—grounding myself was essential to my stamina as I walked (ran), sat, and talked with patients and staff. And it was *essential* to my sanity. Sometimes, I went into a bathroom stall to get a quiet minute and just to feel my feet, my breath, and to recharge.

As a leader, sometimes your facilitation will take place in nutty contexts, sometimes calm; in any case, the "solidly rooted yet light" sensation from a grounding habit can be sustained or picked up again anytime. Really, anytime you're nervous, or too excited to stand it.

(Ha! See what I did there?)

Plus, you've been meditating—you got this.

---

[9] Rev. Rosalyn L Bruyere, *Wheels of Light: A Study of the Chakras*;
Deepak Chopra, M.D, *The Seven Spiritual Laws of Yoga*;
Harish Johari, *Chakras: Energy Centers of Transformation*

In the hours before, and during your facilitation, stay attuned to the portable charging station beneath you. Like a Kegel exercise, no one has to know you're doing it. But if they catch on, what they'll notice is you in good form—fountain of youth (energy) style.

Fill yourself up, walk into the room, give from the over-flow.

Now What

Whether you've practiced grounding yourself and grounding the venue-space the day before, or, in the minutes before you walk in, as mentioned earlier, the space will be ready for you when you step into it. Your grounded-ness will make it easier to maintain the biggest aura among the crowd, and to hold those people alongside your passion *in* your aura[10] for enhanced learning of the subject matter.

Finally, preparing yourself and the space won't solve all your potential tics, but it will help you move gracefully *with* and *through* them so that you can carry on beyond the surprising or frustrating things that come up.

This is also what *biggest aura wins* is about. Make the sacred space big enough to honor everyone; endow it with what you intend.

You're the facilitator. You can and should own that stability.

---

[10] Bio-energetic field which contains your wisdom, knowledge, experiences, intention, and present time emotions and beliefs. Visit: Consciousness and Healing Initiative: www.chi.is

Chapter 16

The Circle

*As women grow older we get more fabulous, gain more
confidence, and have less trouble saying "no." Plus we
have the ability to tap into creativity and pleasure that
many of us never knew during our younger years.*

~Dr. Christiane Northrup, M.D

Setting Up

If you are coordinating your own event, and don't have access to the space for set-up the day before, arrive *at least* two hours before your attendees, especially if it's a new venue. You'll be surprised by how much time it takes to set up seating, arrange your teaching props and then relax so that when your attendees arrive they're not watching you rush around completing tasks, nor experiencing you flustered. If you're using audio visual equipment, you'll need time to ensure that it's working.

Giving yourself plenty of set-up time is professional business practice.

Even in venues I'm familiar with, I typically ask my sister or dedicated students to arrive early to help me with set-up (as I mentioned, I like to offer them discounted or free tuition for this help).

Set-up details vary among venues, activities, exercises and theme, and might include: seating placement with tables, seating without tables, visual props like charts and a white board, food and drinks, program materials, flowers, books...

Setting Up and The Room

In earlier chapters I described my preference to set up participant seating in some sort of circle. While my gatherings are typically 20 people strong, I've facilitated circular Circles with 38. Geometrically, a circle is conducive to a continuous flow of participation because the shape creates a container in which every part of the circle is the same distance to the center point—everyone is equally visible to one another, and with equal opportunity to participate.

Even though I'm not sitting or standing in the center of the circle necessarily, what I am putting there is the subject matter, energetically, for everyone to have equal and easy access to.

I want the subject matter to set the heart-full tone of the gathering when it begins. The circle configuration will help hold it, especially if something is placed in the middle of it, like flowers, books, or sacred nature objects like rocks or crystals.

What's more, as the facilitator, the circle geometry is important to me because not only do I want to have visual and energetic contact with everyone equally (difficult when people are set up in rows—the back row people feel very far away and sometimes less responsible for participating), I want attendees to be in relationship with one another and equally responsible for contributing. We all need to be able to look into each other's eyes, notice body language, and hear one another clearly in order for the benefits of this relationship to have any chance in a group setting.

If you can't form a circle with an intimate group of under 20 people, configure seating so that participants can at least make eye contact with one another.

Even if I'm facilitating a group that's meeting only one time for an hour, if I can make a circle configuration work within the limitations of the space, I make it happen. Better for me, best for them.

How Good a Circle Can Be

Last year, I was recruited to facilitate a long established cancer support group I hadn't known of on the other side of town. It was held in the health clinic waiting room once a month, a place devoid of personality and warmth.

But the health team always provided food and goodie bags and tried to make it very warm. Many participants had family or professional assistance getting to and from the support group; to participants and helpers alike it was worth the effort despite the waiting room sterility.

When I arrived, attendees and staff had snacked and chatted, and were ready for me, their "guest speaker." The overall energy was welcoming and relaxed among this group. Internally, it felt to me like a nice group to be with. But, they were sprawled out over the entire waiting area in chairs set up against walls, a water cooler obstructing view of one other, tables littered with magazines, and more empty chairs between people than there were people in the room.

No matter how nice a group of individuals, it's difficult to facilitate in a disorganized space because other than the walls and floor, there's no container for the teachings or the human connections. A human made container—people seated next to one another—is a very powerful holding tool.

With a light spirit and a joke about my new penchant for interior design, I recruited the able-bodied to help me re-position the chairs and promised everyone they'd like the new circular configuration in ways they can't yet imagine. In four minutes, when all 11 of us were seated together side-by-side and face-to-face, I noticed that those who had been slouching in their chairs against the walls were now, in close physical proximity to other people, sitting up straighter in their seats. Including those with markedly obvious physical challenges. They had become suddenly more present with the group. Invested.

When that happens, participants are also better able to be present with their own feelings.

Before my introduction, I encouraged each person in attendance to make eye contact with the peer on either side of her, these women who they had long supported emotionally. Had been supported by. The staff too. Several in the Circle became tearful. For as many people present, I'm sure there was a diversity of feelings among them about why those moments felt tender and full.

As a group, the space we created within the usual personality-less room, suddenly endowed with a new energy, would never be what it once was: A waiting-room in a clinic where they meet. Rather, it became something fresh—the weeds cleared so that they could be together with more vitality now—dig deeper in order to blossom health bigger. It became a new place with fresh soil to grow their monthly gatherings. Their group had always been endowed, but some of it's richness had been buried in a sterile container.

(I am one big-metaphor lovin' leader, y'all. And, I own it).

The space within the space is your friend. Your awareness will have it working for you.

Chapter 17

Energy, Intention, and Acute Presence Plan

The same stream of life that runs through my veins night and day, runs through the world and dances in rhythmic measures. It is the same life that shoots in joy through the dust of the Earth in numberless blades of grass and breaks into tumultuous waves of leaves and flowers.

~Rabindranath Tagore

Leave Space for Others in the Space, and Establish What You Want Participants to Offer the Group Processes

As facilitators—leaders in service to the greater good—our job description is about encouraging others to shine where *they* exist. But, in order to do that, leader-self-awareness is a crucial tool. We'll always need to "practice" good facilitation even after years of leadership. Each context: Speaking engagement, teaching space, friendship gathering, and holiday family meal, offers opportunities for deeper presence. Self-awareness will become easy and go-with-the-flow-y the more it's practiced up to and beyond the point that Ekhart Tolle often describes in his teachings: You'll be in the moment *and* observing it at the same time.

Seamlessly integrating with your attendees and filling yourself into the space that holds all of you doesn't mean that you are taking up all the space in the room to the exclusion of everyone else's energetic contribution (as evidenced in the last chapter, everyone contributes)—it means that you're encouraging a cohesive environment for everyone's grounding and growth. There's room for everyone to take up an appropriate amount of space too.

Again, I like to use the cherished ancient Jewish wisdom teachings of Mussar as a wisdom map.

The Mussar masters taught that just like the virtue of gratitude, the virtue of humility lives in each of us on a spectrum. On one end of the humility spectrum is self-aggrandizement where a person may take up a lot of space in life physically, emotionally, and energetically. On the other end is self-deprecation and self-effacement where a person feels invisible and doesn't take up enough space in a context. Somewhere along the spectrum there's a happy balance where a person is self-aware and where interactions with others are given room for mutual exchange.

I was a student in a continuing education class last year. The instructor presented some compelling subject matter that I was excited to learn, but she told story after story about herself while demonstrating the exercise. As you know, I'm all about the story telling. However, very few of her stories were related to the lessons on hand. By irrelevant story numero quatro I was irked—it was too much—her tangential talking not only recounted details that had nothing to do with me and my learning, nor anyone else's, they diverted my learning. And they weren't interesting stories.

This instructor's continuous talking took up so much space in our otherwise beautiful venue that I couldn't enjoy my surroundings either, nor feel into my own personal exploration with the exercises.

I'm not saying it was all someone else's fault that my day was ruined, but I am a little bit.

And, I get it. I've been *that* clueless instructor, lacking appropriate humility.

Whether you tend toward taking up too much space when you facilitate (over-sharing), or too little (not enough boundary setting, or charisma or pizazz to make the material come alive) writing your intentions into your Time Map (chapter 12) will provide clear, detailed parameters for you.

Stick to them.

Once your event concludes, journal about your experience. How'd you manage? What can you do differently next time, if anything at all? Where were you effective and how?

Who said leadership would be easy?

But becoming conscious and self-aware is at very least fabulously interesting, and, growing your soul. It's a gift that keeps on giving. Let your awareness be a mission of fascination, and stay away from self-criticism either way. If you can look at your tendencies as interesting, it'll be a worthwhile examination that will lead to positive adjustments toward life skills in other areas of your life, too (we'll examine this more closely in concluding chapters. It's good stuff, I promise).

How to Foster Self-Exploration Among Attendees, and How to Deal with Difficult Emotions When They Show Up (a nice addition to Boundaries chapter 8)

Now that you've assembled a group, you might wonder how to best to: Relate to the individuals within your group, foster a relationship that empowers, ask the "right" questions, respond rather than react to big emotions or surprising personal revelations, and, be a source of stability in a space of shifting perspectives.

Well, you've come to the right book to do that.

In my chaplaincy internships I learned the hard way, all about the art of relationship *with other.* Yes, I did. They've become priceless lessons that I'm very grateful for today (not so much back then).

But, the hard way really can be a good passage for leaders to walk right on through.

In my earliest interactions with patients, their families, and their health-care teams, you can image that all I wanted to do was ease the pain of their overt and subtle suffering. I had a lot of energy back then, especially in the early internships. And I believed that because I knew "a lot", had been trained enough in wisdom teachings to be allowed to serve as a source of support for people, that I carried in my emotional and spiritual arsenal a bunch of answers and experiences that would easily assuage their suffering.

Easily? Nope.

The problem was my approach: "wisdom and a bunch of answers" and wanting to use them instead of practicing being an "active listener." A solid presence.

I'll share with you how active listening provides a sacred presence in you and through you; it's exactly what helps alleviate suffering (theirs and yours in the moment), and is the very balm that reaches toward the soul and touches it lovingly.

"Doing" less is best. Which is the opposite of what most people are tempted to do.

The *less* here applies to all kinds of interactive contexts for one-on-one conversation as well as small and large group contexts, and luckily, also applies to personal relationship contexts (including with friends and loved ones).

You are welcome.

Here goes:

People don't want to be told what their feelings mean.

They don't want to be told that, *"This too shall pass."*

Nor, *"You will get over this."*

They certainly don't want to be told to, *"Get over this."* Ever.

(Don't worry, I've never said that to anyone.)

(Outside my family.)

(I really hope.)

But I have spoken some of the following reactive rescuing statements (yes, out loud.). They're popular among people trying to help. I've also been the recipient of some of these by well-meaning compassionate "helpers". They are NOT helpful and feel terrible to the recipient.

Here they are:

God has his reasons. (Uggh).

You'll be stronger from this. (Ichh.)

This is happening because there's a higher purpose for your soul's growth. (Eww.)

This is happening so that in your suffering, you will be among those you serve. (Ikk.)

The pain and learning from this will be a good thing, you'll see. (Ack!)

What part of you asked for this? (Don't even get me started.)

God doesn't give you more than you can handle. (Especially hate that one.)

And finally, probably the most popular platitude across shitty-things-that-happened-contexts, including on reality television: *There's a reason for everything.*

Big ouch.

No one, including you, wants to be told any of these things when struggling. You'll be more useful and will sound wiser when you simply say, "It sounds like that was very difficult," or, "I'm listening."

And mean it.

The Acute Presence Plan is More Than Cute

It took hours and hours and weeks and years to learn that despite my good intentions and training, I could not in fact alleviate anyone's suffering through the fine art of platitude-ing—could not control what or how others feel no matter how desperately I wanted to help.

But finally, when I let go of that rescuing desire, and showed up to be acutely present to someone's pain or personal discovery, or celebratory feelings, things shifted. I gained trust and eased suffering that very way. In chaplaincy, as in some other service fields, this emotional/spiritual intersection with other is called: *meeting people where they are* (you'll remember from Chapter 15).

One of my favorite bedside facilitation memories comes from my second internship in 2003 in a trauma hospital involving an elderly devoutly Christian woman. That day, I was determined to *do* less, listen more, and truly follow this patient's cues about what *she* wanted to talk about and how—instead of worrying about the potential silent spaces in our conversation.

Importantly, I resolved to not "fix" her pain—whatever it would turn out to be.

So with her welcome to sit next to her bedside, we began a conversation that she directed. By fixing *less* I could ask *more* relevant questions that helped her discover her own answers. And, I could be silent at times, not rush to say anything, sit in the silence with her. I needed to be deeply present in order to do all that, which meant common old responses could not be relevant here.

The effect was very positive; I could tell that she felt supported. And my shift in intention helped me feel grounded and alive in that interaction in a new way.

The way I showed up to this woman's bedside helped create a shared space between us; a sacred one for us, both.

More than noticing it and feeling that it was true, the confirmation came from my patient when she reached for my hand. Holding it she said, "Thank you dear, for being such a good Christian woman. You have helped me so much today."

I thought: *Hmmmm!*

Precisely because I happen to be a Jewish woman and not a Christian one, this articulation was a gift to me—the truest confirmation that I'd hit the mark this time. For her, our intersection felt so familiar and sacred, she assumed I was just like her: Christian. I met her where she was so that *she* could re-align with her own soul where she could feel *herself* and God more deeply, as the space was held for her to do so.

Every facilitator—holding a sacred space for others—does more by doing less.

You are most of the way there as an effective active listener who responds rather than reacts, just by being a witnessing presence to someone's presence—no matter what they're going through, and without hoping to change a thing.

And if just before reading this, you reacted rather than responded to someone, gave them the well-intentioned gift of a banality in "Everything happens for a reason" style, forgive yourself, and move on. I had to. Many times. Until I could relax and stick to the acute presence plan.

When you know different, you can do different. *You* were not wrong, only your reactive behavior was. Your good intention was in the right place, and now it can be in the right place with better responses, including less reactive "helping" statements.

The best leaders are willing to learn from personal foibles, practice self-compassion, pick up, dust-off, and change direction. Sometimes an apology is in order, which is excellent practice in good leadership, too.

Active Listening Techniques Before Verbal Response

It will be clear to you, and to the speaker, that you are listening deeply when you:

1) Try to let go of your attachment to doing or saying something *for* her so that she can be okay, and so that you can be wise. Or heroic. Or the one who "just always knows what to say." Before you speak, ask yourself the reason for your words.

2) Let go of your attachment to the notion that the expression of big feelings is awkward. For her. And you as witness. And everyone else witnessing.

3) Your body has a language that makes your listening effort clear too: sit up straight, hands relaxed. Nod your head yes when appropriate. Feel it out.

4) Pay full attention to the speaker by not looking at anything else in the room while she is talking or processing her revelations and emotions.

5) Make direct, natural eye contact with the speaker. Sustain connection through her processing aloud, including crying. Though you may believe it "awkward" to witness her pain so intensely, it will not be awkward for her to feel safe experiencing her emotions if you are calmly present and fully holding the space for her to do so. You're not gawking, you're making soul to soul contact, even if she's looking down. Your calm holding presence will lead other witnesses in the room to be calm-caring-non-attached-support presences, too.

6) Be comfortable with the speaker's silent pauses—she might have more to say before you respond. You just have to feel this out in the moment.

There will be times in your event when a participant isn't necessarily experiencing a big emotional trigger, but is creatively exploring a revelation. Along the lines of these *active listening techniques* and responses, you might restate the speaker's original statement, and ask a qualifying question. Active listening works in both situations:

Speaker- "I just realized that for the past decade, I've had a fear of commitment, but couldn't completely acknowledge it."

You- "This revelation has come to you just now—that you haven't been able to acknowledge a fear of commitment?"

Speaker- "Yes, exactly."

You- "Can you say more about that?"

Restating not only demonstrates that you grasp what has been shared and can hold the space for it firmly and tenderly, it also provides the speaker with a powerful reflection of her own exploration, and opens the door for more. Sometimes, when a speaker says something out loud and it's repeated back, she can hear herself in a new way because her words become a mirror of *her* own truth finding. It's a very good facilitation tool and your use of it will get easier and easier.

Where as trying to *fix* a person's struggles with analytical "wisdom" makes you a reactive rescuer, a responsive confidant who builds trust and empowers is a responsive listener. You might memorize and employ some of the following deep listening responses until they come more naturally:

"I hear you."
"Help me understand what that feels like."
"That sounds hard."
"I feel moved by this."
"I'm listening."
"I'm sorry you went through that."
"That sounds like a powerful realization."
"I have felt that way" (if you have)

And, I want to give equal attention here to another deep-presence possibility. If you are holding space for someone to engage in an exploration process (such as in SoulCollage®), responding even just with empathy sounds such as "m-hmm" or "aww" can interfere with the personal exploration. In this case, your job is even more simple: Without A Peep, hold the container for *their* inner work. Again, just be acutely present and allow her processing to unfold naturally.

Mum's the word (but not out loud).

Open Ended Questions

"Can you say more about that?" is also an example of an open-ended question. In addition to my earlier points, open-ended Q's are especially helpful because they can't be answered with a *yes* or *no* but require a detailed response based on the speaker's knowledge and feelings, which opens a path to exploring them. These types of questions encourage more meaningful responses. It's important that the facilitator (whether the retreat leader or a peer in a partner exercise) not interrupt, prompt, nor lead.

When I'm asked open-ended questions by a facilitator, therapist, friend, or my husband, not only do I feel I've been given an invitation to look inside myself for some gem, I feel too that my questioner is truly interested in holding the space for me—waiting for me while I search myself—and then stay with me when I get there.

What a gift. Especially in a world where time is a commodity now.

A facilitator who can do this is one I tend to trust and want to go back to time and time again.

More Examples of Open-Ended Questions:

Can you help me understand that better?
What do you feel this means?
What are you feeling right now?
Why is that important to you?
From this realization, what would you like to happen now?
How do you feel about that now?
What do you feel led you to this realization?
What do you want to do about this now, and how do you see that happening?
What is the support that you need?
What do you need from me and the group right now?

Your Participants Working Together

If you incorporate small group exercises, the guidelines above in Active Listening Techniques, and, Open Ended Questions, can be printed and given to your participants (including those situations that call for a peepless holding-the-container response). Call the whole thing something like, *The Effective Listening in Partnership Guideline*. They'll appreciate the hard copy.

Or, you might call it, *The How to Avoid Rescuing Responses or Fumbling Around with Terrible Hokey Platitude Listening Skills at The Expense of Your Peers Guideline*. But that's a long title.

More Benefit Than You Can Imagine

As you now know, I like attendees to work together, and I suggest peer engagement techniques for your facilitation. But this isn't just about the sisterhood vibe inherent in my events where a dynamic exchange takes place between people, which aids in personal discovery through the celebratory supportive relationship.

Not just that.

It's also so that I can hold the space, not micro-manage it. And very much about avoiding a perception of being the magic answer leader in the room.

And most importantly, my intention for participants to work together through their personal exploration, is so that through partnership and group dynamics, participants become empowered to find *their* personal answers in a community context while there.

Whatever the theme of the day, make your leadership goal to: Cultivate a strong foundation for participants' personal exploration within the group. And to open the *way* toward the healing tools that stand on that foundation so that participants feel their own focus and the courage to discover their own answers.

There Really Is an Energetic Affect on Others from *Your* Feeling State

In measuring the electromagnetic field of the heart (using an EKG), science shows us that the heart is 60 times greater in amplitude than the energy of brain waves.[11]

With a critical connection to the brain, the heart is the broadcaster of your energy field so that when you speak, your words have gained power and meaning directly from the energy of your heart's intelligence. Your brain helps formulate your words, but your sentiments don't come from your brain.

It helps to articulate for yourself ahead of time exactly what it is that you feel when you *imagine* yourself facilitating and doing your thing. This is a good way to utilize the logic of your brain with your heart—they are complementary powerhouses; your opening comments should sound appreciative and excited, not sappy.

In my opening remarks with a group, as I sink into my seat (grounding myself), and after I become aware of what I *feel* as I experience the presence of my assembled group, I articulate it as I make eye contact with everyone.

Last year, I led a workshop at the Public Library in my hometown. It was called:

Introduction to SoulCollage®: A Workshop for Women in the Art of Joy.

The program director who recruited me to facilitate said that she would post a registration deadline but that I shouldn't expect a high turnout since free-to-the-public library events tend to suffer the no-show fate, (but that I'd be paid my hourly rate either way).

---

[11] HeartMath Institute: Science of the Heart: Vol 1 (1993-2001) Exploring the Role of the Heart in Human Performance: An Overview of Research

I know all about this no-show thing. Believe me. But I also know that I love to facilitate, and that I especially love SoulCollage®. And that there are now nearly 100 women in my hometown who also really like SoulCollage®. That there's enough energy around all these facts that this library event could be something better than the program director warned me about—that it could potentially have a higher than usual turn-out.

And if not, *oh well*. It would be terrific no matter what because those who attend will help make it special, I'm being paid either way, and, I adore the library system and the wealth of good it brings to community.

I was all in.

So I sent up a little prayer that the library's event description page would attract women who would not only enjoy SoulCollage®, but would benefit from the Women's Circle, and then be excited to take home some new tools for well-being.

A little miracle followed.

Well, two actually.

23 women showed up. 23!

The library's typical attendance is 5-10 people!

And the second miracle came once we were assembled in a big circle of tables adorned with supplies for our workshop, after my introductory remarks, when I articulated the following intention statement for our time together:

We're 24 individuals of diverse backgrounds and experience and yet, we share so much in common as women as a whole. And here this afternoon, we're all are seeking the very same thing: To joyfully explore our theme of joy; To celebrate the feminine spirit in a supportive-accepting-of-one-another-way; To learn something new; To take home and use what is learned.

After the around-the-room introductions that followed, just 20 minutes into the workshop, just 20 minutes in (!), women who knew not one other person in the group articulated versions of the following:

(Since I abide by confidentiality, I'm offering similar sentiments shared aloud, but not the actual statements):

"I don't usually feel comfortable in groups, but I'm feeling really good right now."

"I've never done something like this before, but it feels really nice in here."

"Listening to all of you talk about joy makes me feel really good suddenly."

"I'm really excited to be here—you all seem like a great group of women."

Intention Speaking Is Like Prayer, It's Powerful, and Non Religious

Bringing into the space an articulation of the group intention—especially because initially, participants are not responsible for articulating it, you are—will take you and your group to a greater height in your initial bonding. Intention Speaking is a sacred action, and for those of you who pray, you might recognize a resonance with the power of this. Speaking intentions aloud is a powerful thing.

AndBut, about Intention Speaking, I want to make a clear point here: Unless you are facilitating with a specifically religious group, you should never, ever use language that has any kind of religious connotation to it. You don't want to alienate anyone.

(Even in my chaplaincy roles as a support group facilitator among mostly Christian women, I hardly ever use the name *God* to refer to the essence of God—even though I personally resonate with this name. Instead, I say Higher Power because there is sometimes one person in the room who isn't Christian and doesn't resonate with the use of *God*. By the same token, I'd never use the name *Great Spirit* in a specifically Christian context.)

Notice that when I spoke my intention-setting-statements to my assembled group at the library, nothing I said sounded dogmatic or aligned with any faith tradition. But what I expressed had a powerful impact (obvious from the way participants articulated how they felt just 20 minutes into our gathering after little more than group introductions). It might not have sounded like a traditional prayer to those assembled, but when I spoke and infused heart and soul into my words, internally I felt a resonant, ceremonial, sacred prayer-like fullness.

When I do have more than 90 minutes to facilitate a gathering, I like to invite participants to articulate how it feels to hear the Intention for the day, to hear about how our interconnectedness will serve our event. That becomes a sweet sisterly sharing experience. Interestingly, I didn't even have to ask this group full of newcomers to the Women's Circle—they shared anyway.

But no matter how much time we have, I always ask participants to basically introduce themselves so that their voices are added to the group energy, and so that each participant gets a feel for the others she is spending precious time with before the program begins.

Confidentiality and Trust

Whatever the circumstances of our time constraints or exploration with the material, after articulating the constructive intention of the gathering, I always ask participants to agree with a nod of their heads *yes*, that whatever stories are shared over the course of the gathering, stay in the space we're creating together, and that participants are are free to talk to friends about their personal experiences and revelations after the gathering, but the specific stories of others are never repeated.

I look directly at each participant to witness her head-nodding *yes*. And participants are witnessing this among one another too. If someone is looking down as I go around the circle with eye-contact, I'll say her name and ask, "Yes?"

This is an important verbal and physical contract to have made clear within the sacred space of your gathering.

As the facilitator, you're doing your part to build a general trust among your attendees for their benefit. And eventually, when you direct them to work together in their smaller groups, you will also give them specific instructions for how to interact together to process the subject matter. This might be verbal, or a hand out with clear instructions of the questions they should ask one another.

After providing your adult participants their guidelines, you have done your part and it's enough—trust that you've set the right tone and the groundwork. The rest is for these adults to be responsible with. You can not oversee and monitor every conversation among your group, and most of the time, it'll all work out just fine. If it doesn't, hopefully you'll be advised through the use of the feedback forms (more on feedback forms coming up in chapter 19).

If you've been professionally trained to facilitate tools that have therapeutic efficacy (like life coaching, SoulCollage®, yoga, body work, mastermind groups, writing, art...), you should make it clear that the purpose of personal exploration in this context is NOT therapy, while it is in fact therapeutic.

And, the small group guidelines are an aid to continuing "reasonable" sharing expectations and maintaining appropriate interactive boundaries.

If you've been marketing your event with accurate details, participants will know that there will be some dyad partner sharing or small group processing; knowing what to expect will aid their willingness with one another around partnerships and around comfort being "seen and heard" by others who might be "strangers."

Chapter 18

Miracles, Get Your Miracles

*Every blade of grass has its angel that bends
over it and whispers, "Grow, grow."*

~The Talmud

Synchronicity, Coincidence, Serendipity. Chance. They're Clues!

If it *is* your desire to elevate your facilitation and your events to the level of sacred, it will help you greatly to keep your eyes wide open to the special things—little and big coincidences—when they show up.

In February 2016, in my first year hosting a radio show in my city, when I was at times feeling insecure about whether it was "all synching well", whether what I offered (as the producer and host) was resonant with the needs of listeners—whether I was doing a good enough on-air job—I received a happy little sign that helped me let go of my doubt. And to see that another word for coincidence can be *miracle*.

My guests, two of my favorite holistic health professionals, Wendy and Catherine, who didn't know one another—Wendy a medical practitioner and Catherine a therapeutic body worker—showed up to the radio station wearing almost exactly the same outfit.

And hello, another amazing synchronicity: **I matched both Wendy and Catherine!**

That's right. We three. Same clothing. Nearly identical fitted scoop neck t-shirts in solid black. WHAT are the chances of this among three women in a tiny room?

Synchronicities (and all the names for them) are naturally occurring events that aren't controlled or manipulated by human design, and because of this and the fact that they're unusual, they are compelling.

For the most part, synchronicities are about your life and the way you live it and how. And what you are attracting into your life.

Whether synchronicities are joy inducing like my example here, or the opposite (like, you sprain your ankle and get fired in the same hour) co occurring events are a symbolic and physical clue about your general perspective. What happens around you and "to you" offer pause to stop and pay attention to the great *right now*—to the thoughts, feelings, perspectives that have been driving behavior and actions.

Coincidence calls you to be with what has been going on, to recognize a pattern, and some *cues*, because there's always a pattern to our physical, emotional, mental, and physical tendencies. And those tendencies show up as experiences in your life. Coincidence is a gift to help you realize that you should adjust your thoughts and beliefs, or, to keep on keepin' on.

I've grown up with Oprah in my ear and eyes. I was 22 in 1989 when her first show aired. So it's sometimes her compelling voice that I hear in my head, which sounds like this:

> Your life whispers you warnings and direction all the
> time, but if you don't listen to the whisper it gets louder.
> If you don't listen to that whisper giving you a clue that
> something isn't good for you, that warning turns into
> a problem, which becomes a crisis, that turns into a
> disaster. Eventually it's like your whole house crumbling.
> If you'd only listened to the whisper—that direction—it

*might have only been a little thing in your foundation to
have to fix at all.*

Happy cues or house crumbling ones, stop and examine how *co
incidents* are a whisper or an exclamation point from the Universe
that you *are* on the right track, or, that you are *not*. In my radio show
example, the pattern recognition—the cue—of three women wearing
nearly identical clothing helped me see the exclamation point of right-
track-ness that day. It was the truth that my women's show: The Women's
Well: Nurture Your Health and Spirit, was in fact resonating with my
audience, "matching" interests.

And, though my intention for the show from the beginning was to
match listener's needs, what I didn't know when I was intention setting,
was that the show would yield unexpected gifts: The show would also
resonate deeply and provide sustenance for the expert guests who would
arrive to tell their stories and share their wisdom.

In the same way our listeners benefited from the programming, we too,
as the programming providers—facilitators—become energized by what
we offered in the presentation of it. It was a wonderful miraculous effect
that I classify as significant.

On the surface, matching t-shirts might have looked unrelated to the
content of our task—presenting holistic wellness strategies in self-care—
but it's much easier for miracles to slip into an experience when we've
no expectation of what they might look like.

Need a sign? Ask for a sign. Don't get picky about what the sign will
look like. Instead, remain playfully open about unusual synchronicities.
I say: a miracle is a miracle. And I'll take a delightful miracle however it
shows up, including as a triple solid black scoop neck t-shirt(s).

The Aftermath Is Rich With Symbolism

The symbolism of that "co incidence" tickled all of us in the moment, and continued over our hour together—you can see it in our photo on my website.[12] But to understand the message of a synchronicity, to examine how *co incidents* are a whisper or an exclamation point from the Universe that you are on the right track, or, that you are not, requires a little perspective. It was later in my quiet hours, when I had some distance from the events of my day, that I could sit with it, review and unpack the wisdom of the symbolic message.

Synchronicities are full of symbolism. Stay conscious enough to notice.

Call It

In one yoga teacher training module I facilitated, I read aloud Eknath Eswaren's introduction and translation of the Upanishads (a sacred Hindu text):

Now and then, a sparrow darts in for refuge from the weather…

Our lives are like that…

We spend our days in the familiar world of our five senses, but what lies beyond that, if anything, we have no idea. Those Sparrows are hints of something more outside—a vast world, perhaps waiting to be explored. But most of us are happy to stay where we are. We may even be a bit afraid to venture into the unknown. What would be the point, we wonder?[13]

Can you guess what happened shortly after this introduction to the assembled students?

A bird darted into the yoga studio. Yes, it did.

---

[12] www.LisaMillerBeautifulDay.com, February, 2016

[13] Eknath Easwaran, Introduction and Translation of The Upanishads (Canada: Nilgiri Press) pg.7

After 15 minutes of trying to wrangle it out the door—once we all calmed down again—you know I called it to the group: "A symbolic miracle."

Staying conscious to synchronicities serves you well; as the leader who articulates and celebrates them when they occur, those under your influence and care are served.

Elevating the Awe by Sharing It Intentionally

As the facilitator, you are the chief notice-er and sacred space holder. Take notice, make notice. Go into your gathering lightly holding the possibility that miracles will show up because there's a resonance between the vibes and thoughtful good intention of your service, and the vibes of your event, which seeks to provide perspective for others.

And this applies to your general life outside the gathering space, not just within your professional one.

Not long ago, a dear SoulCollage® friend, Tatsiana, invited me to a house that her fiancé bought. There, she showed me the first SoulCollage® card she'd made (using random magazine images I had supplied) the year before at one of my afternoon retreats.

The card was propped up on the white mantle of the100 year-old red-brick fireplace in the dark-wood living-room. She had placed it there for effect.

Major effect.

You see, this card was a spectacular match to the room we stood in. Like the room itself, the card depicted the white mantel of an old red-brick fireplace and dark-wood living-room.

Her fiancé had unknowingly matched his new historic house to the cozy life-style dreams she actually visualized and articulated for herself, a year before.

She couldn't wait to show all of this to me. We stood in wonderment over it together. She had enjoyed the awesome miracle for several weeks already by that point (and I say *awesome* with full weight here); sharing it with me, someone who joined her in the awe of it, elevated the miracle once again.

The miracle shared, got better and better.

We hugged and marveled and felt the magnitude of this cue that she was on the track between what she wanted and what was in fact happening—what she was living. We both felt the gravity of gratitude for the synchronicity that her fiancé would find a house with features that she dreamed of (from "random" images that came from a magazine cutout that he didn't exactly know about).

It was my friend's miracle but I benefited too! I loved knowing I had been a planet in the atmosphere of that miracle.

You are a leader—a facilitator of healing: STAY AWAKE TO MIRACLES. They are everywhere.

Notice the matching t-shirts, the timing of darting little birds, and the old white-mantel red-brick, dark-wood living room fireplaces. Help your participants gain conscious awareness of "hints of something more."

And as Oprah puts it, listen for the warning whispers too. .

Chapter 19

Logic and Information Are Your Friend

In fact, if you are committed to your own growth, you won't even want your struggles to end because they are the very pathway to growth.

~Alan Morinis, Everyday Holiness: The
Jewish Spiritual Path of Mussar

Feedback Forms

D ear reader, after the last chapter about synchronicity and miracles, the idea of feedback forms might seem blasé, but I promise, they hold some magic too.

Here's the thing about them: THEY WILL HELP YOU become the facilitator of your own dreams. Who doesn't need help? Even the Dalai Lama travels with a crew. I imagine they steer him from potential pitfalls, report to him the highlights and the lows of the day, make sure his tea is hot.

Consider your feedback forms part of your crew. And maybe you should make yourself a nice cup of tea while reading them.

Preparing the Form

Prepare a simple form ahead of your event. What do you want to know about how your attendees felt about your gathering? What do you really want to improve?

Word it so that you can find out what they liked, and what they didn't. That's basically it. Feedback forms are YOUR tool for getting the inside scoop.

All your participants will give you the scoop, just hand their inner thoughts right over, when YOU make time at the end of your event for them to be filled out. There's no other time for it. It's end of event, or lost to the wind, my friends.

Depending on the feedback I'm seeking, my feedback form look might look like some version of the sample below, and I leave PLENTY of blank space for the writing of detailed answers. About five questions are plenty and not overwhelming. For your consideration I've provided many more than five here:

Feedback Form
Name of the Event, Date of the Event

Dear You,

I value your feedback and will use it to improve the programming I can offer you and others. Please answer the following five questions with as much detail as possible. You may remain anonymous or choose to sign your name. If you write a testimonial, please sign your name.

Either way, thank you for taking the time to fill out this form.

With gratitude and chocolate,

Lisa

- Please list the specific things you enjoyed about this Gathering, and say why you enjoyed them.

- Please list the specific things you didn't enjoy that much, and say why.

- Did you notice any "Aha!" moments over the course of your experience? What were they?

- Were there any times during the Gathering when you felt tired, or noticed a lag in the programming? Give details please.

- What new skills have you gained today, and how will you use them outside of this class?

- How did you feel about the partner exercises? Please be specific.

- If you have a suggestion or request for future programming, please list here.

- How would you describe this event to a friend? Would you allow me to use this description as a testimonial to encourage others to experience what you did today? If so, I'm grateful, thank you! Please sign your name to this form; I'll include your first name and last initial in your testimonial.

1) Again, if you want feedback, this will likely only happen within the structure of your event. Ideally, you want and need feedback immediately following your program when it's fresh in the hearts and minds of your participants, and so that you can review it within days of your event which is still fresh in your mind too. Fresh feedback is honest and most accurate feedback. It will help you determine your next moves—even if your next event is scheduled a few months out, or a year out, because what you learn will plant seeds of change and creativity that will remain just under the surface of your consciousness. And solidly on top of it before you're ready to grow and evolve your program.

I sweated a little, the first time I passed out feed-back forms. Waiting patiently in a separate area of the gathering space, I pretended to not be concerned. And pretended to only casually glance over from time to time. It was a long 15 minutes to wait. Later, reading them was not terrible, in fact, most comments were very positive, and I tended to agree with the constructive criticism offered.

Including comments like the following:

It would help to have more time to transition between activities, and more time to just relax with the material presented.

Feedback, no matter what it is, should feel to *you* like your honest friend who wants to help make you even better at what you do.

2) Ideally, if you want to issue feedback forms (and you might not need to for every single gathering once you trust your curriculum, unless you are part of a bigger organization that requires feedback from your facilitation) you should leave 15 minutes of dedicated time at the end for attendees to fill them out. You must account for those minutes within your time agenda. You can't expect people to stay longer than the time of your advertised gathering.

Any less than 10-15 minutes, you'll run into incomplete forms.

3) Don't be a looming presence, or make clean-up noise while attendees try to concentrate on filling out the feedback form; they require space and quiet respect to do so. Instruct them to place completed forms in a pile on a table surface while you stand or sit at a distance. Consider leaving some little chocolates there (I love a good old colorfully wrapped Belgian chocolate single truffles variety pack!). I also like the idea of little folded up fortune notes in a bowl to grab on the way out. It's a nice touch. And good business.

Don't Be Scared

Many new and seasoned facilitators feel some fear asking for feedback—they worry that negative feedback will derail their confidence—that they won't want to facilitate too soon again after that.

But really, as I just mentioned, feedback is your friend. And there will be some very positive feedback alongside some suggestions for doing things differently—which by the way are feedback suggestions, not feedback directives. You are the decider of how things will go at your gatherings. If I hadn't felt the feedback valid, that my transition times were rushed, I wouldn't have made any changes. But as a new facilitator, I *had* been semi-aware of the rushed energy during transitions, just not fully.

You are always the ultimate decider of how things will go next time. And next time. And next time. But it always helps to know how people are experiencing what you offer. It allows you to put yourself in their shoes.

Non-Attachment (Yes, Again!), the Value of Self Review, and Don't Get Caught up in Praise

In earlier chapters I discussed non-attachment to outcome. Again, non-attachment isn't about not caring how things turn out, it's about being less attached to how something will be *judged* by others, and is more focused on doing *your* best, all things considered.

This applies to non-attachment to the gold star ratings as well as to the other ones—the dreaded brown—the not so good ratings. The positive feedback is very nice, but let it be valued information similar in nature to the constructive criticisms or "negative" bits, rather than puff pastry for your ego.

In an interview with David Letterman, Ellen DeGeneres said that she doesn't rely on the rave reviews of her stand-up because if she lets herself believe the intense praise, conversely she'd have to give equal value to the intense criticism.[14]

And whose version of the very same performance is correct anyway?

Taking positive feedback *very* seriously leads to trouble because the degree to which you are carried away by "great feedback" is the height from which you'll fall when you receive feedback that isn't so great.

And, as a facilitator, you don't want to come to *rely* on positive feedback as your marker for doing a good job—it can make you a tail-chasing dog, or worse, a slobbering, vulnerable needy one. Don't be.

Trust Yourself

Using various perspective tools of analysis, you can determine that you're doing a good enough job without relying solely on the approval of others. Constructive criticism has a very different energy and intention from "approval." The former will involve your own thoughtful examination through the following: Journaling, prayer, discussion with your mentors and peers, discussion with your colleagues, discussion with your sister who convinces you to stop obsessing already, and, your feedback forms.

And, if you're serious about improving your facilitation skills, one more very, very helpful tool:

An audio recording your event.

I hear you cursing and groaning over this consideration. All the way over here it sounds like, "Bloody f#*/n hell, WHY??!!! Aaarrrgggggxxxxxxxx. Cough cough cough."

Bubbalah, I hear you! I know how much that hurts. I used to feel the same way.

---

[14] On Netflix: My Next Guest Needs No Introduction, Season 2, Ellen DeGeneres

Now cut it the f#*/ out.

Sincerely, this is not a case where someone is prescribing a medicine that she would not in a million years take, herself. I took that one, over and over, for nearly two years when my radio show was on the air. I played back every single show I hosted—listened to the audio sound of my own annoying voice.

The first few minutes of my first playback was tough ONLY because I anticipated that it would be. And I avoided it pretty well for three days before mustering the courage to review it. To even approach my audio play-back I had to basically gave myself a quiet padded room: I waited until I was alone on my reliable, safe, familiar, living-room couch when the sun would be shining warmly through the window, and with pen in hand, I talked myself into a courageous resolve to "learn from all my mistakes that aren't necessarily idiotic ramblings, but true opportunities for growth."

But because I was producing and hosting a weekly show in the early months, I didn't have *more than* three days to be too chicken to observe and review myself before going on-air again.

Well.

I was shocked to discover that it wasn't too bad. Pretty solid, actually. My fear about hearing myself—reliving my "performance"—was a monster created by own mind. And though my action plan was to take notes that would *inform my habits and style next week*, I made only two minor notes alongside several positive elements of my on-air persona.

The positives were obvious to me *with* the minor things that I could tweak. But noticing the positive things held me up while thinking about tweaking other things. When I could truly listen for the full scope of the experience, the adjustment was easier to contemplate. The "good" things I could claim and own served to empower me.

After that day, the positives that I noticed became the reliable and pervasive support structure for every plan moving forward as a facilitator on the air. And in the classroom, and conference, and podium, later. I can handle both truths: The positives about my facilitation, and the things that require readjustment—the gold stars, and brown.

I bet Ellen DeGeneres does read some reviews, just doesn't let them define her worth.

Tools

So, consider using the voice memo feature on your cell phone to record yourself when you facilitate. You can casually let your participants know that you're recording yourself for personal improvement. Turn on your voice memo recording and forget about it. If you attend to it frequently during your event, your participants will become self-conscious because you are. Just turn it on and move on.

All your review tools provide you the means to "collect enough data" so that you *can* trust your own assessments while leaving room for feedback.

Compliments: Stand There and Take It

And by the way, when positive feedback comes your way, whether written or verbal from attendees, or from your own review, TAKE IT IN. Absorb it into your cells and let it merge with the Light of your soul. That feedback is vital information about how you are being experienced by others, and most often, it's given sincerely. It is not to be ignored, or tossed away. Do not be coy, and don't demur. Don't destroy the moment by shaking it off and saying that you don't deserve it; don't make your complimentor feel she has to justify her feedback or regret offering the gift. That's not nice. Nor professional.

On the humility spectrum, there's a big difference between the desperate-for-attention slobbering pup, and the standing-solidly-on-your-two-capable-feet-looking-your-complimentor-directly-in-the-eye person.

Gracefully accepting a compliment is a practice in emotional intelligence and spiritual maturity. Whether you read it from a form, or hear a voice mail message, or it happens face-to-face, if someone is gifting you with feedback in the form of a compliment, honor them with a *thank you* and some moments of allowing it into your being from theirs.

And because you might be truly surprised by feedback that feels overwhelmingly positive, it's perfectly reasonable and quite lovely to ask a clarifying question of your complimentor. You might say:

> *Thank you So and So, tell me, what did you like about it?*

> *Or,*

> *Thank you, tell me, what makes you feel that way?*

> *Or,*

> *I value your feedback, tell me, how do you think you'll benefit from that (experience, exercise, revelation from the workshop)?*

Or, just say thank you and live your life.

Do not express your doubts to this participant, attendee, student, mentee. If you do, you will effectively erode some (if not all) of the trust you worked to build with this business client.

Cut it out.

If you need to explore your doubts, do so with your mentor, or colleague, or peer. But realize, if you had doubts in the first place, the compliment should be the answer to it—your time to let doubt go. Why cling to doubt after feedback comes your way that you were on the right track?

Consider any compliment to be feedback. But after taking it in, allow it to dissolve like a grain of salt in your overall recipe.

I bet Ellen does that too.

Emotional Health When Brown-Star Feedback Is Intense

When my parents were school aged kids, a red star meant excellence, and a brown one, not so much.

There will be times when a brown star rating feels like a punch in the stomach. It hurts. SO very much. Again, your consideration should be about an examination of your practices and what you might want to do differently next time. OR NOT. Someone's review might be off. Consider the source. Is this person a reliable, stable judge of something?

Either way, harsh feedback is not, should never be, EVER be, about an examination of your worth as a human being. Because that's not what the feedback is about—negative or positive. Even if an attendee wrote: "This is about you and how wrong, bad, and stupid you are," the comment is still not about you, it's about a feeling-state that *they* experience—probably live in continuously—and are bothered by.

When my daughters were little and they did something they shouldn't have, I tried to be very careful to use feedback words and energy that avoided character-judging corrections. I really wanted to focus instead on addressing the "behavior" that was undesirable.

REALLY. REALLY. REALLY. A LOT.

I tried.

Even so, a loving Mommy who adored the souls and personalities of the tiny offspring, I found it challenging to not be childishly blame-y in that there case.

The truth is that grown adults sometimes have immature ways of expressing dislike, discomfort, or distaste. Do not, I repeat, do not, allow some criticism to bother you on repeat in your head for eternity. Or even a week. More than two days of upset is a signal from the *mental health stability* center of your being that you need some objective support with it. With the help of a therapist, I have always found more courage to look at something difficult, especially if I feel guilty or responsible for something. Off and on, this help has served me profoundly for over 20 years of my adult life.

Good mental health hygiene will always make you better in your professional life. You are not separated into distinctive parts. Each area of your human being-ness overlaps with every other and serves every other part of you. It's all life. And it's all always about growth and joy.

Just as philosopher priest, Pierre Teilhard de Chardin, put it: "We are not human beings having a spiritual experience. We are spiritual beings having a human experience," when I've been able to see my most difficult personal and professional challenges as rich with learning, they have served *me* profoundly. I don't want to waste one misstep or tragedy; if something devastating happens, better believe I'm using *it*, not the opposite.

Look, some will like your leadership facilitation, some won't. Allow yourself the following internal response, and feel it: *What I offer is not for everybody.*

You don't love everyone else's style and offerings either.

Chapter 20

The Sweet End

Every new beginning comes from some other beginning's end.

~From the band Semisonic

The Closing Circle

Whether we're sitting or standing in a circle, or rows, or a square, I adore the closing Circle—it's more a point of closure than a geometrical shape. Closings are important because they gather the harvest of the event where human beings have come together for the purpose of healing and growth, and allow the magnitude of all that to feed its participants before departing back to routines.

Especially in a small event, it's a way of identifying the harvested fruits that belong to each participant so that her gifts aren't left unclaimed and later forgotten by her.

Along with the circumstance of the gathering, a participant's ensuing awareness of her gifts is a special occasion—I'm referring both to the gifts of her own unique strengths (her revelations, and also what she contributed consciously, or not) as well as the elements of the event gifted to her. It can be how *the sacred* emerges in a personal way for each person in attendance.

And that's wonderful. But beyond how special that is, it's also magical because what is articulated in the small closing Circle—shared—by each participant about herself, her learning and inspiration moving forward is not just for the participant herself, it's also for every other woman in the space who suddenly hears *her* own unique empowerment and inspiration through the articulation of someone else's.

And, it gets better yet again: Whether shared with one other person or within a group context, there's a built in utility in speaking aloud what's in the heart—bringing it to the open space of possibility outside the physical and energetic body to be released into the world. Into the world of a participant's reality it goes so that it can be transformed from something *in the process of becoming,* toward something in the *process of existing.* Out in the open it can be noticed and attended.

All of this can best be described as the intersection of the sacred with the mundane—which makes it a quintessentially human intersection; no matter how elevated the experience, and magical and God endowed, the sacred is precisely meant to be a gift that is used in every day life— through the muck and desperation and tears, just as thoroughly as through the confetti and bliss of a special occasion.

In small to mid-sized groups, I frequently call-in the ritual of the closing Circle this way:

Briefly in a few sentences, each of us can articulate a take-away, or a new little seed of personal understanding or inspiration from your experience today. Or most importantly, articulate a hope and goal moving forward. There's no pressure: Pass or play.

Not everyone closes a Circle with articulated take-away-s, some leaders offer wordless ceremonial closings with beautiful music and movement, like my wonderful mentor in the SoulCollage® organization, Mariabruna. Her presence holds an energy of cohesion for individuals to reach inside themselves for the conscious knowing while the group wordlessly stands in support and celebration.

Play with closings, you'll find the style you love best in your own facilitation.

Timing

If I'm facilitating an afternoon event, or days long, I typically leave 45-60 minutes for a closing Circle. If it's a shorty event, just 90 minutes-long or so, I'll save a little time for the *closing Circle sharing* at the end of the gathering.

All of those precious allocated minutes are important. Be aware that the closing Circle minutes aren't taking time away from the meat of the program, they *are* part of it. Almost anyone can drop a bunch of supplies or techniques in the middle of a room and encourage participants to use them; what makes *creating a sacred space* different, is the conscious processing of the richness of being together in community using those supplies.

Whether articulated or wordless, the energy of the closing Circle is key.

Gratitude and Honoring

Aaaaaahhhh. You've done it—pulled it off—gathered people and provided programming. Some things worked, some not. But either way, *you* were there and grew through it all—even if you're not yet clear how.

And now your attendees have filed out and the space is empty.

But it's not truly empty.

Because it's true that people gathering for the purpose of learning and growth and opening themselves to the clarity of their wisdom, and others' *was* the transformative element that elevated your event from a get-together, to a sacred gathering. And if you pay attention once you are alone in the very space that held that—that helped *you* hold that—you will feel a pulsing fullness there contained within the walls and floors and ceiling of the place. You might have been too busy while facilitating to notice when it happened, and when it enveloped the group, but now is the time for noticing that it became a holding container.

And that calls you to pause. To acknowledge and respect it—to give thanks for it—even if you have only 30 seconds to do so. Because it is big. Don't miss out on it, or the truth of your *co-creation* of it, that you helped to make the sacred possible through the initial seeds of your hope, and through the hours and hours of heart-full co-creation of it.

Yes again, co-creation, because you've never been alone cultivating the seeds, the hope, and the hours and hours of heart-full effort. You've had help, lots of it from Life and the intelligent creative forces of Life.

Whatever that force looks like, feels like, sounds like to you, it was always whispering in your ear. Maybe you call that God, or Higher Power, or Great Spirit, or Guidance, or angels, or creative non-local intelligence, or grace (or Big Enchilada in the Sky). Whatever that it is for you, it's been the wind through you.

You've had help with all the details that lined up in your favor. And when they didn't line up, you weren't alone in your disappointment. Maybe from an unexpected obstacle, a new way to do something emerged.

Corny or not, you must know it.

Later, there will be time to honor and maybe even feel gratitude for that which did not work well, but in the private moments before your exit, the important thing is to feel into the general, pleasing, happy truth of what did.

If it's not possible to say "thank you" aloud in the space before I exit, I scan the entire room, from corner to corner, floor to ceiling—this takes mere seconds—and I say it inside.

Acknowledging what's in the heart, will take what's *becoming* into *existing*. That goes for deep thanks, too.

It's no accident that the direction of this book began in gratitude, the presence of gratitude in the planting of seeds to make something grow, and that it ends with gratitude now too. Here's gratitude again, sitting in the conclusion buffering the very end of it.

Gratitude is a full-cycle human virtue that you should take into all your Afterwards.

Afterward and Afterword.

The Garland. Evaluation. Begin Again:

This is a space that's calming, celebratory, honest, kind, fine-tuning.

Chapter 21

Time to Celebrate, and How Did My Prep Tools Hold Up, Serve?

Joy is what happens to us when we recognize how good things really are.

~Marianne Williamson

Honoring

I t's time to honor the occasion of your event with a symbolic gesture. Do this right after, or a few days later.

Why is an honoring gesture (or ceremony, call it whatever you want) important? Because from the material resources, to the people, and the grace of invisible support, to your own training and fortitude, your event grew from a seed that reached down deep to make supportive roots and then moved up and along as an emerging shoot, and eventually blossomed into your finished goal. People came together!

People were brought together because of something you cultivated: a sacred space.

And that is really something special.

From seed to harvest, all of these elements—unseen, visible, inanimate, and human—contributed to the fact of completion of your goal. So, considering what was involved, to the degree of effort you and others and forces greater than you put into this event, an honoring gesture not only properly shows gratitude for what worked beautifully, it completes the cycle of creation. Because the process of the creation was a significant one.

Wisdom traditions from around the world have always demonstrated the importance of this acknowledgment—ancient scripture is full of examples—and this continues through every corner of our modern world. Any farmer involved in a harvest festival will tell you so. Nothing that grows is ever taken for granted or forgotten after its use.

So, a little ceremony, or action, is a gesture of appropriate thanks and completion. And leaves you in a position of integrity and consciousness for the exchange.

Honoring Nourishes the One Who Honors, Too

Proper thanks and honoring are also celebratory occasions which continue to "feed" the one who honors. Look at the decorated hut of Sukkot, or the Ganga Aarti ceremony on the Ganges River, or the adornment of the Christmas tree. Look at full moon celebrations of old, or moon celebrations anywhere in modern day—even from the NASA science lab. Or, hear the mesmerizing heartbeat drums of an Indigenous tribal gathering anytime.

We humans continue to get so much out of honoring, appreciating and celebrating.

But this responsibility need not overwhelm. If you're not resonant with big gestures of thanks, your act of gratitude doesn't need to be a BIG thing for it to be a sincere offering.

If you are a thank-you-note writer, or have ever received a note of thanks, you'll identify with the meaning and relative ease of this completion cycle. With a little more effort, you can plant flowers in a public place—symbolic of thanks that others will benefit from—rather than in your own garden for your edification. Or another idea: Buy and donate clothing and basic essentials in honor of your success. Or make a monetary contribution to an organization or non-profit.

Sometimes I write a poem that no other human sees but that I hope God and my Spirit Guides hear.

Often, I stand in my kitchen and simply light a candle on my counter and speak my thanks aloud while looking at the trees and sky out the window over my sink.

Upon reading this, one of my editors, a self-confessed candle guy himself, asked me if the depth of a thanks-gesture impacts its lasting effect. The answer is *yes yes yes*. Gestures don't have to be big or take a lot of time, but depth counts. You should engage your symbolic thanks-gesture when you have time and aren't rushed. If you mean it with a whole heart, and you offer it with gratitude, humility and joy, whatever gesture you choose will impact your next event. It will impact you (and God, of course), and will impact those around you, lastingly.

Choose something that matches you. Sweetly, this afterward time will complete the cycle that you yourself started from your Idea Seeds, and will feed and sustain you in the completion.

Gratitude Grows More of What You Want

Even if this is the first "event" you've completed, there have been countless other times in your life when you've created something, made something work, turned toward an exciting new direction. And have you noticed that among the times you celebrated and spent in gratitude, that they became more and more, in some way?

After the first Girls Rock! Workshop, I didn't know if there would be another. I wasn't sure people wanted it, so I decided to be patient. In the meantime, the celebration of our workshop accomplishment was thorough. The teen mentors and the professional team reveled in an article about us that came out soon after. I talked to the parents who were delighted with the program. I held a debriefing meeting with my professional team over lunch—the dedicated volunteer pediatrician and nutritionist. Lunch turned into a meeting endowed with shared awe over the little and great benefits of our event. The adults became teary over the joy of such a good community program. I took in the praise and congratulations from my family over the success.

Our dwelling in celebration led directly to the continuation of the program. Dwelling in what worked led to incorporation, to forming a Board of Directors, and to becoming a non-profit. But in the beginning, all those developments weren't necessarily in our perspective—they grew from our gratitude and celebration and eventually, from our inspection of details we could improve.

Beginning Again

The beginning of this Afterward time, with its focus on *honoring* and *gratitude* is certainly about the full-circle cycle of asking, action, receiving, and thanks and celebration, but it's also about the steps into beginning again—back to where you started, thinking and feeling into what you'll grow next.

And, the focused thanks for what worked even in the midst of what didn't will make more satisfying things-that-work for next time. If you're familiar with the Law of Attraction, you know that's how it works: Energy flows where attention goes.

Everything on this planet—humans, animals, plants—grow and expand in beautiful ways when adored. Look with adoration at what you created!

While everything in your facilitation experience deserves your attention, and you should sit down with your original goals to discern how things worked out, the bulk of your focus should be spent on what went well. Those beautiful things will help you solve the problems and will simultaneously grow the entire desirable thing up to its full potential.

Chapter 22

On Your Way to Mastery

The only difference between a flower and a weed is judgment.

~Wayne Dyer

Review, Mistakes, Grace, Humor

Directly following the honoring and gratitude time—the celebration of what worked and knowing what you want to grow more of—you should feel brave enough to look beyond your feedback forms for what you can improve. This is for the purpose of growing your wisdom, a helpful element in the heart of your personal and professional business as you move forward.

The truth is that no matter how clear and focused your own intentions, as mentioned in chapter 17, things come up. Or when you need them to, they don't—like the door to the venue won't open with the key the owner gave you yesterday before he left town. Or you drive 30 minutes out to the country to facilitate an eight-hour training and leave your notes on the kitchen table.

In the midst of shit like that goin' down, it will help you dearly to say to yourself out loud:

Things usually work out for me. This will pass. What do I need to do in this moment to help things along?

The Heart of Leadership for Women

Be Your Own Private Eye

And later, sandwiched between your feelings of gratitude for what worked to your advantage, and planting new seeds of desire moving forward—right in between—should be your honest, clear, fearless analysis of your entire event. Worts and blooms and all.

Write it all down in your Idea Seeds Journal, not just to get it out of your system, but to investigate, which is much easier to do when it's in bullet point on a page.

Let yourself become an objective investigator.

So what now?

Louise Hay, an inspiring 21st century leader in consciousness was famously known for living personal responsibility authentically and was a proponent for honest, but loving self-talk. She has helped millions of people reframe their perceptions.

In the opening pages of her beautifully crafted, You Can Heal Your Life, she says:

> *Life is Really Very Simple. What We Give Out, We Get Back*
>
> *What we think about ourselves becomes the truth for us. I believe that everyone, myself included, is responsible for everything in our lives, the best and the worst. Every thought we think is creating our future. Each of us creates our experiences by our thoughts and our feelings. The thoughts we think and the words we speak create our experiences.*[15]

As a friend, dear reader, I ask you this:

---

[15] Louise Hay, You Can Heal Your Life, (Carlsbad, CA: Hay House), pg. 13

Are you mindlessly retelling story after story of hardship to whomever will listen? If you are, your intention in the moments of retelling is likely to entertain, or make conversation, or to generously share yourself in friendship. Or, perhaps it's a habit. But I promise you: Your retelling is keeping your woe, your very pain and problems, very much alive by continuing the telling.

There's a big difference between your initial emotional need to vent and process a painful experience or mobilize forces for positive change in the world—a big difference between that and re-infecting yourself and everyone around you with gunky energy of what happened before now. If you feel the need to bring an old wound back up for therapeutic reasons, find a therapeutic professional to listen. That's the best context for it. As much as you can, refrain from the woeful story telling, unless in the moment, it provides a valuable gift for you and your listener(s).

Because essentially, it's not just *the thoughts you think that are creating your future*, it's your articulation of them that endows them with undeniable staying power. Growing power. Whether you're articulating something personal, professional, or about someone else's life, Louise Hay truly leads us here in becoming mindful of not inviting the energy of past misfortune into the right-now.

Your business life and your personal life will reward you for your conscious effort to focus upon and say aloud more of you want, and less of what you don't.

Paradox Is for the Sacred Space Makers

Here we are with the mystery and thrill (yes, thrill!) of paradox once again—spending some dwelling-time with the juxtaposition of things that worked right alongside things that didn't. Embracing the weirdness of that allows balance on the spectrum between avoiding responsibility for how things turned out, and self-blame.

The truth is that you can't always be completely conscious of your role in how and why something went down. As much as we like to believe we can access all the deepest and highest parts of ourselves, there is a well of mystery about life and the facets of our souls. We are after all, multifaceted walking miracles within a miraculous cosmos. Life, dharma, and karmas are all so complicated to human understanding—who can completely grasp it?

This doesn't mean that you should worry about not having control in a swirling universe, it means that you can keep looking with an evaluative eye through a clean optimistic lens, not a worried, whining, or blaming one.

The afterward review of your event—whether a workshop, class, ceremony, conversation, retreat, tour, or performance, is a time to see every mistake not as a misstep, but as a vital step on your path to mastery. And great happiness. Because after struggling with the thing that you're trying to improve, your joy will be superlative.

Superlative!

On the way to superlative, humor will help immensely. That's happened for me. A lot.

A few years ago, on a beautiful summer evening, I facilitated a gathering for women next to a lovely pond in a shady park that is also a nature preserve in my town. The plan was to wrap up by sundown, but alas, though I'm normally very punctual with opening and closing timings, the sun began to set while four out of ten participants hadn't yet shared their "take away" in our closing Circle. And as you now know, closing Circles are a very important component of the gatherings I facilitate.

"The park will be closing in 10 minutes," came the loud speaker announcement. And onward they—the women of my gathering—shared. Because I encouraged it and wanted it to work. And wanted everyone to have her share of attention in the closing.

But within a minute of that announcement, I felt nervous. In terms of time, participants share an average two to six minutes of their take-away in a closing Circle. I began the calculation—which is not a good thing to do while someone is speaking in the best of circumstances—and with four participants to go, and the setting sun, things were adding up. Badly. Minutes ticked away. Two women still to share.

"The park is now closing. The park is now closing. The gates will now be locked. The park is now closing."

"THE GATES WILL BE LOCKED, SHIT!" I tried to sound casual. Gates being locked was a new announcement.

In all my years of facilitating (twelve years by that point) I had never moved so quickly away from a gathering.

"Okay!" I announced, feeling terrible for the two women who were short changed their time to be heard, I jumped up from my blanket in the grass, terrified I might cause everyone severe inconvenience being locked-in. From every square inch of visible skin, I blushed in embarrassment for my poor time management and how I'd need to speed things along now in problem solving mode.

"I'msosorrythatwecan'tfinishproperly, I heard myself say, I'mgonnaRACE totheGatetoMAKESUREitstaysOPENuntilALLyourCarsareOUT tfreeAndclear!"

And I did. Like The Roadrunner on amphetamines through the normally slow four-minute drive from the pond to the gate. I drove it madly in one minute while my group gathered up all the supplies I brought for our Circle back at the dreamy gathering spot: food, chairs, and a table.

You can exhale. I'm trying to exhale just writing this.

I made it to the gate before it was shut, in the twilight, which descended quickly after the last over head announcement. As I put my car between the gate and the lock, until all my people made it out alive, I exhaled.

A little. I was too embarrassed to fully exhale.

Ugghhh. Oy. Ay carumba. It's still a slightly painful facilitating memory. Frenzy and fear is the last thing I want to offer as a lasting impression in the final moments of an event. Especially after such a gorgeous sunset. But, it happened, and it was not the end of the world.

And, it was kind of funny that I looked like a fool.

In SoulCollage®, a renowned therapeutic arts process used in diverse settings all over the world—which you know by now that I love—there's great appreciation for the *role* of The Fool archetype. I didn't know the importance of The Fool yet that night, but would come to appreciate it later.

Turns out, there's great freedom in releasing a fixed idea about perfect endings.

Room for The Fool and Miracles

At that Women's Circle gathering in the park, the presence of The Fool was a gift embedded within our beautiful meeting, and I, the one to embody her and *take one for the team.* Especially because in a Circle where the themes revolve around self-discovery and living from the core of being, health and wellness, and finding and maintaining life balance, The Fool had provided a teachable moment: To go with the flow of the FULL life recipe there—the peaks and the pits, and moving *with* all of that—how circumstances unfold as life does its thing.

A favorite typical wisdom teaching from Abraham-Hicks:

> *Going with, rather than against, is always the path of least resistance.*[16]

And, if you can't be a graceful Fool while swearing like a pirate as you race to the gate, you certainly can be once you get there (after you exhale and inhale again). And especially once on the other side of it.

Especially then.

Because it as it turns out, The Fool archetype can morph into A Swan—graceful—gliding through water even when it's choppy.

You are the leader and facilitator, the role model in closest proximity to those attending your event; making light of your imperfections is not only important for those you lead, it is vital for you. Offer the impression you most want people to have of you—that you are a credible professional, and, one who sometimes makes mistakes. And then you must believe it yourself.

Before I calmed down enough to realize entirely that my foolishness would have the opportunity to play out into graceful swan-hood, I emailed everyone and apologized, especially to the two women short changed in the closing Circle, and in my apology, made light of my goof. In and of itself, an action like that is graceful.

But importantly, on the other side of the gate the next day, contacting my participants helped them to move on, too. I'm sure everyone already felt bad for me and my mistake and my silly ungainly exit. Or maybe they didn't and I made it more important in my assessment of that gathering. Either way, I didn't want to make my participants feel my embarrassment by dwelling on it unnecessarily.

Truly, non-attachment to perfection will open the door to wonderful possibilities you couldn't have dreamed up or intend, because once you let go of grasping, there's a wide open space for miracles to get in. And

---

[16] www.abraham-hicks.com

my friends, sometimes those miracles are disguised at first to lead you to something important like allowing yourself to be amused with your absurdity, and then letting go of the need to look graceful all the time. This benefits absolutely everyone. Can I get an Amen?

I promise you, your leadership can relax after fucking up; letting go of pride sheds a lot of burden. Though I much prefer grace and ease, the pits are important too. It's all worth it.

Before the beginning of your next event, leaving room for The Fool to show up is an excellent practice in releasing unreasonable expectations, or even a hope for things to be go perfectly. You can intend for your event to go as planned and you'll work toward that of course, but not clinging to pristine ideals will set you free you gorgeous silky water bird, you.

Onward Because You MUST

You are becoming a seasoned facilitator who creates sacred spaces—this is all part of it, it's all good.

Importantly, focus on what worked so that what didn't work can be absorbed into the mulch of your leadership cultivation. At your next event, no matter how long you've been a leader, it will all be less lumpy and bumpy. Because by that point, by virtue of all your efforts combined, you will have elevated your own spirit and openness for leadership and growth. No one will know exactly what you put into the he*art* of the leadership-sacred-gathering-mix. That's for you to appreciate behind the scenes.

What your attendees *will* know however, is that what you're doing is working—that whatever seeds you've planted are growing hardy roots. And now blossoming sweetly, too.

Selected Bibliography and Resources

Bruyere, Rosalyn L. *Wheels of Light: A Case Study of the Chakras.* Arcadia, California: Bon Productions, 1989.

Chopra, Deepak. *Perfect Health: The Complete Mind Body Guide.* New York, New York: Three Rivers Press, 1991.

Chopra, Deepak, Simon, David. *The Seven Spiritual Laws of Yoga: A Practical Guide to Healing Body, Mind, and Spirit.* Hoboken, New York: John Wiley & Sons, 2004.

Csikszentmihalyi, Mihaly. *Flow: The Psychology of Optimal Experience.* New York, New York: Harper & Row, 1990.

Davidji, *Secrets of Meditation: A Practical Guide to Inner Peace and Personal Transformation.* Carlsbad, California: Hay House, 2012.

Emoto, Masaru. *The True Power of Water: Healing and Discovering Ourselves.* New York, New York: Atria Books, 2003.

Epstein, Mark. *Going to Pieces Without Falling Apart: A Buddhist Perspective on Wholeness Lessons from Meditation and Psychotherapy.* New York, New York: Broadway Books, 1999.

Eswaran, Eknath translation of *The Upanishads.* Canada: Nilgiri Press, 1987.

Frost, Seena B. *SoulCollage® Evolving: An Intuitive Collage Process for Self-Discovery and Community.* Santa Cruz, California: Handford Mead Publishers, 2012.

Gandhi, Mohandas. *The Story of My Experiments with Truth*. Victoria, B.C: Reading Essentials.

Goldner, Diane. *Infinite Grace: where the worlds of science and spiritual healing meet*. Charlottsvile, Virginia: Hampton Roads Publishing Company, 1999.

Goleman, Daniel. *Emotional Intelligence: Why it Can Matter More than I.Q.* New York, New York: Bantam Books, 2005.

Hanh, Tich Naht. *No Mud, No Lotus: The Art of Transforming Suffering*. Berkeley, California: Parallax Press 2014.

Hay, Louise. *You Can Heal Your Life*. Carlsbad, California: Hay House, 1999.

Hicks, Esther. *Ask and it is Given: Learning to Manifest your Desire*. Carlsbad, California: Hay House, 2004.

His Holiness The Dalai Lama, Cutler Mark. *The Art of Happiness: A Handbook for Living*. New York, New York: River Head Books, 2009.

Johari, Harish. *Chakras: Energy Centers of Transformation*. Rochester, Vermont: Destiny Books, 1987.

Kabat-Zinn, John. *Wherever You Go, There You Are. Mindfullness Meditation in Everyday Life*. New York, New York: Hachette Books, 2005.

Kornfield, Jack. *Meditation for Beginners*. Boulder, Colorado: Sounds True, 2008.

Kshirsagar, Manisha. *Ayurveda: A Quick Reference Guidebook*. Twin Lakes, Wisconsin: Lotus Press, 2011.

Kshirsagar, Suhas. *Change Your Schedule, Change Your Life*: Harper Wave, Chicago, 2018.

Leadbeater, C.W. *The Chakras*. Wheaton, Illinois: The Theosophical Publishing House, 1927.

Morinis, Alan. *Everyday Holiness: The Spiritual Path of Mussar*. Boston, Massachusetts: Trumpeter, 2007.

Myss, Caroline. *Anatomy of the Spirit: The Seven Stages of Power AND Healing*. New York, New York: Three Rivers Press, 1996.

Northrup, Christiane. *Women's Bodies, Women's Wisdom: Creating Physical and Emotional Health and Healing*. New York, New York: Bantam Books, 1994.

Orloff, Judith. *The Empath's Survival Guide: Life Strategies for Sensitive People*. Boulder, Colorado: Sounds True, 2018.

Rosenberg, Marshall. *Nonviolent Communication: A Language of Life-Changing Tools for Healthy Relationships*. Encinitas, California: Puddle Dancer Press, 2015.

Rovelli, Carlo. *Seven Brief Lessons on Physics*. Great Britain: Penguin Random House, 2016.

Schiffman, Erich. *Yoga: The Spirit and Practice of Moving into Stillness*. New York, New York: Pocket Books, 1996.

Sri Swami Satchidananda, Translation of *The Yoga Sutras of Patanjali*. Buckingham, Virginia: Integral Yoga® Publications, 1990.

Taylor, Kylea. *The Ethics of Caring: Finding Right Relationship with Clients for Transformative Work in Professional Healing Relationships*. Santa Cruz, California: Handford Mead Publishing, 2017.

Tolle, Eckhart. *The Power of Now: A Guide to Spiritual Enlightenment*. Novato, California: New World Library, 1999.

Zukav, Gary. *The Dancing Wu Li Masters: An Overview of the New Physics.* New York, New York: Harper Collins, 1979.

Zukav, Gary. *The Seat of the Soul,* New York, New York: Simon & Schuster, 1989.

Abraham-Hicks daily inspiration newsletter: www.abraham-hicks.com

A Network for Grateful Living: www. gratefulness.org

Ayurvedic Healing: www.AyurvedicHealing.net

Center for Action and Contemplation, Richard Rohr's daily newsletter: www.CAC.org

Consciousness and Healing Initiative: www.CHI.is

Frost, Seena B. *Facilitating SoulCollage® in Groups, Audio C.D.* Santa Cruz, California: Handford Mead Publishers, 2010.

Louise Hay daily affirmations: www.LouiseHay.com

On Being with Krista Tippet: www.OnBeing.org

The Chopra Center for Deepak and Oprah's free meditation challenge: www.Chopra.com

The Mussar Institute: www.mussarinstitute.org

Lisa M. Miller is an expert group facilitator—especially for women—who brings to life perennial wisdom that provides the compass for a life of meaning and well being today. Through a diversified, holistic career spanning two decades, she's emerged as an internationally recognized champion of mind-body health. She's married to Jonathan, her summer camp sweetheart of over thirty years, and is proud of their adult daughters, both inner city teachers, and leaders themselves.